A NORTHERN FRONT

**BOREALIS
BOOKS**

A NORTHERN FRONT

new and selected essays

JOHN HILDEBRAND

Borealis Books is an imprint of the
Minnesota Historical Society Press.

www.borealisbooks.org

The Minnesota Historical Society
Press is a member of the Association
of American University Presses.

Manufactured in the
United States of America

10 9 8 7 6 5 4 3 2 1

∞ The paper used in this publication
meets the minimum requirements of
the American National Standard for
Information Sciences—Permanence
for Printed Library Materials, ANSI
Z39.48-1984.

International Standard Book Number
978-1-68134-068-5

*Library of Congress
Cataloging-in-Publication Data*

Hildebrand, John.
    A northern front : new and selected
essays / John Hildebrand.
    p.   cm.
ISBN 978-1-68134-068-5

    1. Human ecology—Alaska.
    2. Indigenous peoples—
       Ecology—Alaska.
    3. Human ecology—Middle West.
    4. Nature—Effect of human
       beings on—Alaska.
    5. Nature—Effect of human
       beings on—Middle West.
    I. Title.

GF504.A4H55 2005
304.2—dc22   2005001140

Acknowledgment is given to the following publications in which versions
of these essays first appeared. From
Harper's Magazine: "A Northern
Front," © November 2003; "The Appraisal," © November 2001; "Coming
Home," © October 1998. All rights re-
served. Used by special permission.
"Snow on the Mountains" and "Wolf at
the Door" were in *Sports Illustrated.*
"Following Hemingway" is from *Out-
side* and "Touching Bottom" appeared
in *The Missouri Review.* "Beyond
Whales" and "In a Far Country" ap-
peared in *Mānoa* and "Deer in the
Tree" and "Looking for Home" were in
Harrowsmith Country Life. "Wolf Re-
dux" and "On Being Lost" are from
Audubon and used with permission.
"Fables" is excerpted from *Reading the
River: A Voyage down the Yukon*
(Houghton Mifflin Co., 1988; repr.
University of Wisconsin Press, 1998).
"Fences" is excerpted from *Mapping
the Farm: The Chronicle of a Family*
(Alfred A. Knopf Co., 1995; repr. Min-
nesota Historical Society Press, 2001).

The quotation on p. 36 is from "Proud
Mary," written by John Fogerty for the
Creedence Clearwater Revival and re-
leased on the album *Bayou Country,*
January 1969, © Fantasy Records.

All italicized passages in "Wading the
Big Two-Hearted" are from Ernest
Hemingway's "Big Two-Hearted River:
Part I–II," in *The Short Stories of
Ernest Hemingway* (New York:
Charles Scribner's Sons, 1938).

This book is for Rachel and Jack

A Northern Front

Preface

A few years ago, I was lucky enough to spend time aboard the *Alpha Helix,* a research vessel operating in waters off southeastern Alaska. I'd been invited along on the cruise in the capacity of "guest naturalist," though I had no specific duties other than to hang around and watch the marine biologists at work. This mostly entailed looking over the side of a rubber Zodiac dingy at the divers' bubbles rising to the surface and wondering what was going on below. The divers were making transits of the sea floor and counting sea urchins, which they brought up in net bags. There were lots of sea urchins in the area because there were no sea otters, not yet anyway. Urchins are the otters' preferred food. When otters move into an area, they eat all the urchins they can lay their hands on, and this alters the underwater environment because urchins feed on algae that would otherwise support a different host of creatures. An area with lots of sea urchins is typically a barrens while an area with sea otters tends to be a kelp forest. One day I cornered John Oliver, the chief scientist aboard, and asked him to explain the point of the research, the bags of urchins and so forth. He said, "We chase stories," which seemed a strange thing for a scientist to say. What he meant was that his crew was assembling different pieces of information—so many sea urchins per square foot of sea floor— that by themselves didn't mean much, but put together might reveal something greater, a cause-effect relationship. In other words, a kind of narrative.

I like Oliver's phrase for its modesty and precision. It's what I've tried to do in the twenty-odd years over which these articles and essays were written. To chase a story is to admit from the very beginning that you don't know where it's going. You stumble around taking notes, putting scraps of information into your net bag, and hoping that somehow all the details will coalesce into a meaningful pattern: a story.

What does it take to make a story? Events, character, a theme. A novelist can invent a character to order, but the journalist must go out and find one. My main requirement is finding someone who can write his own dialogue. Words not only make the man, they shed light on one's field of expertise. When I wrote about my wife's family farm, some of my father-in-law's language seemed rooted in another age. How else to explain expressions like "Christ O'Friday!" or "Putting the kibosh" on something? Agriculture, like most areas of specialization, has its own terminology, which can be precise and occasionally poetic. To know that a "heiferette" is a bred heifer or that a "moon-blind" horse has a milky eye or that the field where the cows go after evening milking is the "night pasture" is to go a long way towards glimpsing a private world.

There's a certain freedom in realizing that you don't have to be the center of attention, that a first-person narrative can be a framework connecting other people's stories. My first large-scale experiment in this kind of writing was a summer-long canoe trip down the Yukon River. It was a homecoming of sorts since I'd moved to Alaska in my twenties and built a log cabin intending to live off the country. Failing miserably at this, I did what many people do in the face of failure—I went to graduate school. A decade later, traveling down the Yukon, I was curious about the people who stayed in the bush and remained faithful to that particular dream. One morning on the middle Yukon I drifted past a white wall tent on shore and a woman on the beach waved, and I waved back. Then she made this motion with her hand, tipping an imaginary coffee cup, and I turned the canoe toward shore. She and her partner were dog mushers who ran a fish camp to feed their sled dogs through the winter. I spent the night on the floor of their tent and we talked about a lot of things but what I remembered best was a story of their neighbor who'd drowned in the river. It resonated with me because I was constantly afraid of drowning myself, and more importantly I recognized how, for the river people, the burial signaled both an end of one era for them and the beginning of another.

Most of the pieces I've written follow a pattern; they start with a landscape and end with people. Maybe it's because I often write about people I don't know. In a literal sense, they are people viewed from a distance, and writing is my attempt to shorten that distance. If "sense of place" implies a particular meaning that can only be decoded after long residence, then I don't buy it. A landscape is both a place and an idea of that place. What interests me is the way people—farmers, emigrants, field biologists, even tourists—project their ambitions onto the same space. The most compelling of these is the idea of home. It's a strange construct of emotions and allegiances—this story we tell ourselves about where we belong—and the conflict between versions often lies at the heart of what I've written.

Long ago I realized that I didn't want to be strictly a memoirist. I didn't want to limit my subject matter as a writer to what happened to me or where I happened to live. I still subscribe to the old-fashioned notion that we share common interests, that our fates are somehow linked. If I wrote about Native villagers on either side

of the Brooks Range or farmers fighting city hall or Hmong emigrants tramping the midwestern woods, it was because I thought
it possible to tell other people's stories without co-opting them. To
take a provincial view of the world is to surrender a great deal of it
to very large, impersonal forces that hold far more sway than you
or I. Writing is a chance to have one's say.

A NORTHERN FRONT

Coming Home

The view from Five Mile Bluff on the west bank of the Chippewa River in Wisconsin extends beyond five miles, so that looking down the gun sights of the valley, one sees across a vast canopy of swamp white oak, soft maple, basswood, and river birch to where tangled bottomland forest gives way to open hayfields and prim white farmhouses with matching barns and the tall Harvestore silos known as "big blues." It is a vista of the kind that kept landscape artists of the nineteenth century busy illustrating such themes as the marriage of wilderness and cultivation or, on a loftier level, a young nation's limitless possibilities. Above its mouth, the Chippewa River splits into two unequal channels: the main channel skirts the bluffs, braiding itself like a glacial stream around sandbars and wooded islands, while Beef Slough, the lesser channel, runs a parallel course to the east before unraveling altogether. Between the channels lies a wedge-shaped floodplain twelve miles long by two and a half miles wide. From ground level—that is, to anyone slogging across it on foot—the Tiffany

Wildlife Area is a dire swamp, a Mesopotamia of deadwater sloughs and pothole lakes interconnected with beaver canals, islands within islands, where the most pressing possibility is the possibility of getting lost. Every year, hunters manage to lose themselves in this pocket wilderness, some more permanently than others.

On an Indian summer day in October 1970, a thirteen-year-old from nearby Durand became lost while duck hunting with his father and older brother. It was the boy's first hunt, a rite of passage in these parts, and he had wandered off in a light jacket and tennis shoes. By evening the temperature had dropped below freezing, and the search for the missing boy intensified. Being lost is usually a temporary setback, more a loss of equilibrium than self, since it's not you that's been misplaced, only the sense of terra firma that comes from knowing where you are in the world. On the other hand, to remain lost for long is to court more drastic synonyms: defeated . . . abandoned . . . departed . . . dead.

"The best thing, of course, is not to get lost," the Boy Scout manual advises in its avuncular way. "But there may come a time when you are temporarily 'bumfuzzled' and don't know where camp is. Here are a few things to do. Sit down on a rock, or under a tree, and think the whole thing over. In fact it's a good time to think of a few funny stories. In other words calm down, and don't be afraid. If you let your imagination run away, you will run away, and probably run in a circle and come right back to where you started."

Did the lost boy sit down on a rock and tell himself a funny story? More likely he let his imagination run away and then gave frantic chase, because three weeks later the boy's body would be discovered lodged against a marker buoy in the navigation channel of the Mississippi River. He must have fallen into a slough and the current carried him away, swept him miles downstream, far from home and all that he would ever know of this world; it swept off his tennis shoes, but a handful of shotgun shells would be found in his jacket pocket. In the painful interim, the search escalated, drawing more and more searchers into the swamp. At one point, more than five hundred volunteers spread out at arm's length to form a human chain and walked the length of the bottoms from channel to channel, bushwhacking through thickets and scaring up deer and a few massasauga rattlesnakes but no lost boy. Sentiment began to turn against the tangled landscape itself. An editorial in the *Durand Courier-Wedge* accused the state of maintaining the Tiffany Wildlife Area as "a private jungle," a metaphor wrong on both counts, though it must have seemed timely, especially when one of the searchers told the newspaper, "I never realized we had a Vietnam so close to home."

These woods have a long memory. Twenty-two years later, Kia Xue Lor, a Hmong immigrant from Laos, lost his way in a blizzard while deer hunting in the Tiffany with his son and a friend. Ten inches of snow had fallen the night before, and the three hunters, none standing much over five feet tall, waded through drifts up to their knees. Occasionally they'd cut a deer trail in the snow, always headed in another direction, but there was no sign of other hunters. About noon, the younger men decided to hunt elsewhere and agreed to meet Lor in the same spot a few hours later. Lor hiked east through a monotonous winter landscape of windfalls and prickly ash until he came to a frozen pond. Circling the pond, Lor assumed he would intersect his own tracks and follow them back, but they eluded him. By four o'clock, the winter sky was darker than the snow-covered ground, and Lor frequently stopped to listen for traffic on Highway 25 to the east. He could see bluffs above the tree line, though he was so turned around now that he had no idea what side of the river they were on or if he'd passed them earlier that morning.

Thoroughly "bumfuzzled," Lor scraped away snow beneath a large tree and sat down to wait for his son to find him. He had no food. His hunting outfit consisted of three pairs of pants, a nylon jacket, and a pair of moon boots. Heaping brush together to form a windbreak, he made a fire and then lay beside it, alternately roasting and freezing. In Laos, he had slept alone in the jungle many times during the protracted war with the North Vietnamese and the Communist Pathet Lao, sometimes drinking a potion made from the bladders of wild pig and deer that enabled the sleeper to awaken at the slightest sound. He had a great fear of waking to loud noises.

The next morning, he followed an airplane and ran into two local hunters, who called the Department of Natural Resources to pick him up. As other members of the search party drifted back to the landing, one ran into a Hmong who said he'd just been threatened in the woods. A local hunter had promised to cut the Hmong man's dick off if he ever caught him hunting in the area again.

"But to return to our back settlers," J. Hector St. John de Crèvecoeur wrote in 1782, "I must tell you that there is something in the proximity of the woods which is very singular. It is with men as it is with the plants and animals that grow and live in the forests; they are entirely different from those that live in the plains. . . . [T]his is the progress; once hunters, farewell to the plough. The chase renders them ferocious, gloomy, and unsocial; a hunter wants no neighbor; he rather hates them because he dreads the competition. . . . Thus our bad people are those who are half cultivators and half hunters; and the worst of them are those who have degenerated altogether into the hunting state."

Crèvecoeur, the agrarian optimist, was describing an America newly wrestled from the wilderness. What could he possibly have made of Buffalo County, Wisconsin, at the twilight of the twentieth century, where the plow is finishing a poor second to the chase? Ever since outdoor magazines began listing it as the top county in the nation for trophy white-tailed deer, farmers have been selling off their hilly woodlots to outsiders for more than the cultivated fields are worth. Working farms are a vanishing act even as blood sport occupies their former occupants. Crowded into public hunting grounds such as the Tiffany Bottoms, the landless locals face increased competition from newcomers like the Hmong and grow ever more "ferocious, gloomy, and unsocial."

On the opening day of hunting season, I saw no deer in the river bottoms but plenty of small men in makeshift tree stands calling to one another in a language as high-pitched and fluty as birdsong. Hmong hunters are easy to pick out: anyone standing five feet tall or so, carrying a single-shot shotgun, and wearing sneakers. Obviously they were seeing deer because there was no end to the gunfire. In the late afternoon, sun low in the trees, I ran into a local hunter climbing down from his metal tree stand after a pointless day. Shrugging off his bad luck, he began to praise, rather elaborately I thought, a Hmong tree stand he'd found in the woods.

"Oh, it was beautiful. Like something out of *Swiss Family Robinson*. Bent limbs for railings going up the sides. A seat fashioned out of a log." He shook his head and winked. "Big wind blew it down." The wink was conspiratorial, because he'd played the role of the wind.

On the way home, I stopped in Durand to chat with a man who had grown up on the last farm in the Tiffany before the state bought up the land and let it revert to swamp. A skilled woodsman, he'd trapped and hunted there all his life, but not anymore.

"My boys and I used to hunt the bottoms the week before Thanksgiving. Got some big bucks out of there. Now I don't even bother. You see *them* at the Ella boat landing in pickup trucks and boats that we paid for!"

A grin flickered at the corners of his mouth when he spoke of the path the DNR had recently cut through the Tiffany. He called it the Ho Chi Minh Trail.

Not wanting to be one of Crèvecoeur's "bad people" who hates his neighbor because he dreads the competition, I drove out to see Kia Xue Lor, the man who'd been lost in the blizzard. He lives in a public-housing complex off a cul-de-sac on the north side of Eau Claire. The decor of these apartments is interchangeable: a few pieces of furniture, school pictures of the immigrant's children, and a black-and-white photograph of a young man, usually deceased, in the slightly operatic uniform of the Royal Lao Army. Lor is a wiry, intense man in his early fifties with slicked-back hair and a few gold teeth. We sat on his living room couch, an interpreter between us, while Lor poured out the past. He had been a soldier all his life, his career following the fortunes of the Armée Clandestine. At fifteen he joined the army, and he fought the Pathet Lao and North Vietnamese for the next fifteen years until the Americans pulled out of the war and left him behind. He knew the Communists would kill him for collaborating with the CIA, so he moved his family into the jungle and for five years fought with a local resistance group before fleeing across the Mekong River. A photograph on the wall showed Lor and his family a month after their arrival at Ban Vinai refugee camp in Thailand, donated clothes hanging in folds around them. After eight years in the camp, Lor came to this country through the aid of a church group, but without English and somewhat disabled by war wounds, he couldn't find work.

A steady stream of kids had flowed into the living room until a dozen or so sat cross-legged on the floor watching a video of Disney's *The Lion King*. Lor whispered something in Hmong to one of the little girls, who announced to the others, in English, "Shut up." I'd considered asking Lor if we could hunt together sometime, but it struck me that a person who must address his children's friends through a translator remains, in many vital respects, lost.

The six-hundred-year-old Kingdom of a Million Elephants and One Parasol did not enter the American imagination until a civil war between Laotian government troops and the Pathet Lao and their North Vietnamese allies turned into a test of the Kennedy administration's Cold War resolve. After the Geneva Accord of 1962 guaranteed Laos's neutrality, operations there became strictly covert, fought largely by a Hmong army of the CIA's own devising, supplied from Air America bases in Thailand, and overseen by case officers with such jaunty noms de guerre as "Bag" or "Mr. Clean" or "Mr. Hog" or "Kayak." It was the agency's largest operation, a secret conflict, a campaign of surrogates that maintained the fiction of neutrality. Former CIA director William Colby called it a "non-attributable war."

In late 1965, a small plane carrying Colby, then chief of the CIA's Far East Division, bumped down on the dirt airstrip at Long Chieng, a remote valley in northern Laos. It was an otherworldly place, surrounded by mountains and weird limestone outcroppings, a thatched-roofed village at one side of the airstrip and a complex of corrugated metal buildings at the other. Colby had come to visit General Vang Pao, leader of the Armée Clandestine. Vang Pao had risen from a thirteen-year-old jungle runner to the highest-ranking Hmong officer in the Royal Lao Army. His hill tribes engaged the North Vietnamese in exactly the kind of guerrilla war that they themselves waged so successfully across the border. During summer monsoons, his army took full advantage of the landscape, attacking enemy operations mired down in the mud on the Plain of Jars, an expanse littered for three thousand years with eleven-foot stone vessels of debatable origin; in the dry season, the Hmong disappeared into the surrounding mountains. Colby, who had parachuted behind enemy lines in Europe with the OSS, understood the value of an irregular force engaged in a limited campaign on their own territory. For him, Laos was a people's war against a foreign aggressor, and in Washington he argued to increase support for Vang Pao. Yet the nature of the war would soon change. "Some immutable principle," Colby wrote in his memoir, "provides that a barefoot guerrilla force must inevitably grow to become a conventional army."

The "immutable" in this case was Vietnam. At its height, Vang Pao's guerrilla army grew to thirty thousand men, with so many CIA advisers that Long Chieng became known as "Spook Haven." The purposes for which they fought were increasingly dictated not out of concern for a "neutral" Laos but to support an expanded American presence across the border. Vang Pao's army tied down North Vietnamese divisions that otherwise would have faced American forces in South Vietnam. Hmong soldiers guarded a secret radar installation, which, until it was overwhelmed, allowed the all-weather bombing of North Vietnam. Hmong road-watch teams attacked the labyrinth of supply lines running along the Annamese Cordillera between Laos and Vietnam known collectively as the Ho Chi Minh Trail. To these ends, Vang Pao's army sustained enormous losses and became increasingly dependent upon American air power and massive bombing. Still, one could argue that the Armée Clandestine was an unbelievable bargain. The CIA spent in a year (Hmong soldiers earned about three dollars a month) what the military spent in a day in Vietnam, and no American boys were being drafted to die in the misty mountains of Laos.

The Chippewa stretches a quarter of a mile across at the Ella boat landing unless the river is cottoned in predawn fog, in which case it seems as wide as an ocean. A dozen of us stood at the landing on an early September morning, poking flashlight beams into the mist and waiting for a boat to ferry us across. In the distance, a cow bawled like a foghorn. While the others joked among themselves in high-pitched monosyllables, I felt myself lost in a dense cloud of language that would part unexpectedly when, for instance, someone boomed into the darkness, "Where are you, Grampa?"

The Eau Claire telephone directory lists forty-nine entries under X, all of them Xiongs. Two generations were represented at the landing, and a third was lost somewhere in the fog. Joe Bee Xiong had invited me squirrel hunting with his family, and it was his father who was missing. When an hour passed and the boat still hadn't appeared, we launched my canoe to look for him. Joe Bee held a flashlight in the bow, illuminating snags and sandbars recently emerged from the river, as we drifted downstream.

Ahead, through tatters of fog, we spotted a skiff dead in the water, its sole occupant straining against an oar. Northern States Power, which operates a series of hydroelectric dams upriver, had cut the flow of water on the weekend to save for peak power demands and, in the process, had stranded Joe Bee's father on a sandbar.

Unlike the *Walpurgisnacht* of the opening weekend of deer-hunting season, in squirrel season the Hmong have the woods to themselves. The Xiongs had carved their camp out of thick brush between the riverbank and the abandoned track bed of the Chicago, Milwaukee, St. Paul, and Pacific Railroad. The rest of the party, having arrived the night before, lounged on sleeping bags beneath a green tarp or else hunkered over a smoldering fire. The older men have the short legs, barrel chests, and sloping shoulders of weight lifters, whereas their teenage sons look lank and reedy—the difference, I suppose, between a youth spent hoeing mountainside fields and one spent sitting in a classroom.

In the montane forests of north-central Laos, the Hmong raised rice and corn by slash-and-burn farming; they also hunted the surrounding jungle at every opportunity. Arriving in this country as refugees, they settled in cities and made forays into the countryside on weekends to hunt. Wardens sometimes arrested Hmong for having blue jays, chipmunks, and robins in their game bags. When the DNR translated its game regulations into Hmong, it was a difficult task, for the language had no written script until the 1950s, no equivalents for such terms as "recycling" or "composting" or "outdoor recreation." The manual jumps back and forth between a taxonomy of the familiar and the strange. Listed under "Protected Species" are "Bitterns, Canada yij Spruce Grouse (*poi yij*), cormorants, cranes, eagles, falcons *thiab plas*, great blue herons, grebes, gulls, hawks, kingfishers, loons, mourning doves, plovers, prairie chickens, ravens, sandpipers, swans, *yam tsiaj uas tsis tsim kev kub ntxhov thiab tsis ntshai.*" In Laos, the Hmong had traditionally hunted songbirds, squirrel, red deer, buffalo, wild pig, and monkey with homemade arrows and bamboo crossbows. In the

1960s, they used M-1s, M-16s, hand grenades—the full arsenal of democracy.

Joe Bee Xiong, his thirteen-year-old son, Lar Zeng, and I followed the railroad tracks south through a canopy of overgrown bottomland hardwoods. At some distance from camp, we stopped so that Lar Zeng could practice shooting his father's new .22 rifle at a maple leaf tacked to a tree trunk. Every time the boy worked the bolt action, Joe Bee would announce, "Safety first!" in a manner so grave and quietly deliberate that it took me a moment to realize he wasn't repeating a hunter education slogan but merely telling his son to push the safety forward so that the rifle would fire.

The first time I met Joe Bee in his office in the Eau Claire County courthouse, where he worked as an employment specialist, he wore a dark blue suit and an American-flag lapel pin. Now he looked dressed for an insurgency in fatigues and carrying armament that included, besides the .22, a shotgun and a bayonet blade. At thirty-five, he was old enough to have fought in the "secret war" against the Pathet Lao and young enough to have graduated from an American high school. It's hard to imagine which was the more trying time. Having shared the defining experience of two generations, he is in the unique position to mediate between the elders, whose lack of English isolates them from the larger society, and the young, who've grown up on TV and hip-hop. As a Xiong clan leader, Joe Bee is responsible for an extended family of more than three hundred, not to mention eight children of his own. He is both a traditionalist who believes the landscape is animated by spirits and a consumer with an eye for the latest gizmo.

"Thirty-five degrees northeast," said Joe Bee, consulting a compass on a lanyard around his neck before we plunged into the woods. The fog had burned off, leaving the forest dappled in leaf-light. For their part, the squirrels stayed hidden or else danced momentarily across the crowns of the tallest trees. Lar Zeng's job was to circle the tree and chase the squirrel into the open so that his father could plink it with the .22.

I didn't see the squirrel until it was free-falling, an acrobat who'd lost his grip, tumbling through thin air to land with a soft *humph* among the fallen oak leaves. A couple more joined it in Joe Bee's knapsack before we headed back to camp. We bushwhacked north through stinging nettles and prickly ash, then along the stinking shore of a deadwater slough caked in duckweed. It seemed a perfect jungle to me. In the distance, we could hear the tattoo of small-arms fire.

How was this different, I asked Joe Bee, from hunting in Laos? "No tigers."

Joe Bee grew up in Mong Cha, a village in Xieng Khouang Province. When he was a child, a tiger came into the village and killed some of the family's chickens. The next evening, the tiger returned and carried off a pig. Joe Bee's father took the boy along to follow the tiger because the older man's hearing had been damaged in the war and he needed his son's ears for the pursuit. Through the jungle gloom they followed the pig's strangled cries until they reached a spur of Phou Bia massif, at nearly ten thousand feet the tallest mountain in Laos.

"I was younger than my son at the time. My father asks me which way the tiger is going. I say, 'That side of the mountain.' My father says, 'That's impossible. Are you sure?' I say that I am certain, but I didn't understand the echo from the mountain. So we lost the trail. The next day we followed the right trail, and all we found of the pig was its head lying on the jungle floor. My father was angry at the loss of the pig because he knew the tiger would keep coming back until all our animals were gone. So he wired a hand grenade to the pig's head. That night I woke up to an explosion off in the jungle. When my father followed the trail the next morning, he found the tiger had lost its head."

In Hmong folklore, the tiger symbolizes evil. It is the stock villain in cautionary tales in which children who wander too far from the village are greedily devoured. A master of guile, the tiger can also appear in disguise or transform itself into human shape to trick widows into believing their husbands have returned from the dead. In a jungle full of bears and snakes, the tiger is the most feared creature not only because of its great strength but because it possesses the dangerous ability to metamorphose, to change it's stripes, to be one thing one day and something else another.

In 1973, Joe Bee Xiong took his father's place in Vang Pao's army at its mountain headquarters at Long Chieng. He was twelve years old and did not look out of place. As Hmong casualties mounted, the army's ranks were filled with boys and old men; most everyone in between was dead. Flooded with refugees from an uprooted rural population, Long Chieng had become the second most populated city in Laos, but the spooks were gone. The secret war, always a shadow of the larger conflict across the border, was winding down. Shortly after signing the Paris peace agreement with the North Vietnamese, Henry Kissinger arrived in Laos to persuade the royalist prime minister to reach a similar agreement with the Pathet Lao. But without the American presence, this attempt at reconciliation collapsed when North Vietnamese troops captured a town in Laos. In May of 1975, Joe Bee, having returned to his own village, heard the news that General Vang Pao and his closest supporters had been evacuated from Long Chieng to Thailand.

The Pathet Lao sent thousands of loyalists—including the former king, queen, and crown prince—to "seminar camps," from which they never emerged. The Hmong in particular were marked for retribution. In the following years, as many as 150,000 fled across the Mekong River into Thailand; others took up arms buried since the cease-fire. The center of resistance was Phou Bia, the fog-shrouded massif whose foothills had once hidden Joe Bee's tiger. After his own village came under attack, Joe Bee went to the mountain to join Chou Fa, the same resistance group Kia Xue Lor had fought with in the jungle, a movement whose leaders claimed to be able to foretell the future and to possess a powerful magic that would protect soldiers in battle. Sometimes the magic worked, sometimes it didn't. In late 1977, North Vietnamese and Pathet Lao forces converged on Phou Bia, bombarding it with artillery and T-28 airplanes. Survivors accused the Communists of dropping chemical/biological weapons on Hmong villages, though corroborative evidence remains sketchy and experts have dismissed the "yellow rain" as everything from bee pollen to defoliants left over from American stockpiles.

Joe Bee, who had escaped the attack by moving to his cousin Doua's village, joined thousands on a month-long exodus south through the mountains and bamboo forests to the Mekong River. A few days away from the Thai border, those who survived ran into a North Vietnamese army patrol, and in the ensuing firefight one of Joe Bee's friends was killed and five were wounded. Scouting ahead of the main party, Joe Bee and a few others reached the river, which stretched more than a mile across, wide enough to dwarf the water buffalo on the other side. Beyond it lay refugee camps and an uncertain future. Centuries ago, when the Hmong lived in China, they had a saying: "If you don't see the Yellow River, your heart will not be saddled." Joe Bee understood this to mean that the courage of ignorance is stronger than the swiftest current. Waiting until dark, the men kicked across, using bamboo poles as floats. For an entire generation of Hmong, crossing the Mekong would be as common and significant an event in their history as steerage passage across the Atlantic was to emigrants of the last generation.

Back at our hunting camp, a pot of rice steamed on a portable gas stove. Tupperware containers of sticky rice and hot peppers lay open on the ground while a young man sat beside the campfire gutting squirrels with a jackknife. There was a whiff of something acrid in the air.

"This is how we cook squirrel," said Joe Bee, and he tossed a squirrel onto the fire, where it smoldered until the fur ignited in a blaze. Turning the squirrel with a stick, he scraped away the burnt fur until the bare carcass was thoroughly scorched. Deprived of fur, the squirrel looked even less appetizing, its long whittled nose and whip-like tail more a caricature of a rodent. It looked, in short, like a burnt rat.

"The smoke," said Joe Bee, "is what gives it the flavor."

The blackened squirrel was cleaned and chopped into pieces before being thrown into a stewpot with red peppers, lemon grass, and ginger root. When the stew was ready, Joe Bee took a spoonful, whispered something in Hmong, then tossed it into the brush. It was a kind of grace before meals, he explained, an invitation to whatever spirits inhabited the woods and a request that nothing bad would happen while we hunted there, though I gathered that the midwestern landscape had nothing on the Laotian highlands when it came to ghosts.

The stew was delicious. We ate it with sticky rice dipped into a pepper sauce that made my lips vibrate. For dessert there were sweet cucumbers from the garden, peeled and eaten like ice cream cones. Everyone ate seconds except Doua's son, who had been stung by a wasp and lay moaning under the tarp, his mouth swollen shut. I felt stuffed, but at Joe Bee's urging I ladled the last helping from the pot into my bowl. Bits of squirrel meat floated anonymously among the vegetables, all but unrecognizable, all but one: a pale globe of bone papered in flesh.

"Ha! You got the head!" said Joe Bee, as if I'd plucked out a golden ring. "The Hmong say: If you don't get the squirrel, you eat the head. The next time, you'll outsmart the squirrel."

It made roundabout sense, the notion of outwitting the thing that you desired by becoming it. Joe Bee, I noticed, had a skull in his bowl too.

The Hmong Mutual Assistance Association occupies a red-brick building in downtown Eau Claire directly across from an autobody shop and the local Jobs Service. In February, the streetlights blink on by late afternoon, illuminating a ridge of dirty snow between sidewalk and curb. Inside, older Hmong sat at a table study-ing to become citizens. The walls are decorated with *National Geographic* photographs of villages perched on mountain ridges, turbaned women in black pajamas pounding rice by hand, fields walled in by jungle—the world left behind. Afraid of losing their government benefits, the older men and women crammed for the naturalization exam:

In order to vote in the United States, a citizen must—

    A. *own property*
    B. *have a steady job*
    C. *speak English clearly*
    D. *be old enough*

Upstairs, a handful of Democratic Party veterans and political innocents, myself included, were mapping out a campaign strategy to elect Joe Bee to the city council. Five seats were up for grabs, yet there was no single compelling issue at stake. The possible excep-tion was Joe Bee's candidacy itself. A Hmong candidate had run for the school board two years before and lost. The good news was that Eau Claire's Hmong community, which had grown from twelve or thirteen refugees in 1976 to nearly three thousand, was solidly be-hind Joe Bee. The bad news was that only a hundred or so were registered voters.

The main question tonight was whether Joe Bee's résumé—family man, employment specialist, former police reserve officer, businessman—should also include his military service.

"I'd strongly advise against it," said an older committee member. "Might put people off, especially in the Third Ward."

The Third Ward is where I live, a university neighborhood where the Vietnam War is still a tricky topic and mere mention of the CIA, no matter how distant the connection, brings an involun-tary shudder. Whether Joe Bee's service was a campaign plus or a liability depended upon the larger question of whether the Hmong were our forgotten allies or hired mercenaries engaged in an illegal war. Either way, the Hmong presence in this country is inextricably bound up with the war, and their cool reception here may reflect the lack of magnanimity one feels toward partners in a failed venture who show up, years later, as reminders of the loss.

On a cold spring night, Joe Bee's campaign workers gathered at the committee manager's home to eat spring rolls and watch the election returns trickle in on the television. The competition included a bank vice president, a realtor, two retirees, and a former assistant superintendent of schools in a race that clearly favored incumbents. At 8 P.M., Joe Bee was in second place. An hour later, he'd dropped to third. The early totals represented only a few districts, so there was still hope. By midnight the tide had turned and it was all over.

Joe Bee received 5,879 votes, winning a seat on the city council and the distinction of being the first Hmong elected to any city office in Wisconsin. He threw a victory celebration at the local VFW, giving new meaning to the concept of "veterans of foreign wars." Afterward, those who'd worked on the campaign were invited to Joe Bee's one-story home near the airport. Tables had been set up in the basement, and the women brought more noodles and spring rolls and sticky rice. We toasted Joe Bee and one another with warm beer: the Happy Toast, the Thank-You Toast, the Welcome the Guests Toast. An old *txiv neeb*, or shaman, wished Joe Bee a life as long as an unending river and the strength of a mountain so that when the wind blew he would remain unmoved. A *hus plig* ceremony followed, each of us tying a cotton string around Joe Bee's wrist for his good luck. I was happy because my candidate had won. Joe Bee, a solid cuff of cotton strings on his wrist, was happy despite having taken on even more responsibility. But Yong Kay Moua, head of the first Hmong family to settle in Eau Claire, seemed the happiest.

"It really means that this is our hometown. We came to America twenty years ago, and we've been waiting for some word, for someone to say, 'Your home is our home. Welcome.' This election shows that this is a hometown for the Hmong and not a temporary place."

Four days after the victory party, somebody smashed the right side windows of Joe Bee's Toyota van. The next night, the left side windows were broken and, for good measure, a window on his wife's car. The evening after that, someone shot out a window of Joe Bee's younger brother's car with a pellet gun. Police staked out the neighborhood, but after two nights without incidents they left.

Blind routine in the face of reason is a hallmark of the chronically stupid. Late the following night, two men were trying to rip the plastic off one of the broken windows when they were surprised by a group of Hmong spilling out of Joe Bee's van, in which they had been taking turns as lookout. Joe Bee's brother chased them while the others called the police, who stopped a red Dodge Omni shortly after 4 A.M. The driver of the Omni was a twenty-year-old white female; her accomplices were seventeen and nineteen. Eventually, police linked the trio to twenty-three cases of criminal damage to vehicles and eight cases of theft from autos, but clearly they had felt something special for the Xiongs.

The classic struggle in American society is never competition for the top—a foregone conclusion—but the kicking and shoving over who will occupy the bottom rung. Fear of personal slippage drives the most outrageous acts of bigotry. "The chase renders them ferocious, gloomy, and unsocial." The immigrant is despised not for his cultural differences—his strange language and impossible cuisine—but for driving a better car. The Hmong, however, are unique among immigrant groups in that the cold shoulder they sometimes got may be linked to our own ambivalence about Vietnam. Perhaps the teenagers who trashed Joe Bee's car had absorbed the dark brooding of adults who could not bear strangers returning home in place of sons and brothers lost in the war.

Yong Kay Moua, who'd reached Eau Claire before any of his countrymen, understood the frustration better than most. "Maybe you didn't come home with the same people but with different people. Different color. Different size. Different shape. Maybe coming this way changes their faces. Maybe you were expecting someone else, but some people came back and you should welcome them."

In late May, Joe Bee attended a convention of Hmong war veterans in Fresno, California. On the last day, he joined nearly five thousand middle-aged veterans in camouflage fatigues performing close-order drills on the playing field of Cal State's Bulldog Stadium. A handful of ex–Raven and Air America pilots flew T-28s over the stadium in the missing-man formation, a gesture that couldn't have been more relevant to the men on the ground. They were an army in exile, parading before the flag of a kingdom that no longer existed. In this country, nationalism gives way to ethnicity, which soon becomes memory and finally ritual. Even if the Communist regime falls in Laos, few Hmong of Joe Bee's generation would be returning except as tourists.

The event had been billed as Lao Veterans of America Recognition Day, but it was largely self-recognition. Ex-CIA personnel and former Air America pilots showed up, but few of the invited government officials. The most noticeable absence was the late William Colby, whose presence was evoked by a makeshift shrine in front of the dais that held photographs, a bowl of fruit, and the blue shield of the CIA. The man who had kept the agency's operation in Laos a secret for so long spent his retirement trying to make up for that anonymity by speaking to Hmong groups across the country. One might argue that he was as responsible as anyone for the Hmong being here instead of there. Colby had planned to attend the conference in Fresno but had disappeared two weeks earlier while canoeing on the Wicomico River, a tributary of the Potomac. For eight days he was presumed lost until searchers discovered his body floating in shallow water half a mile from his vacation home. Apparently, he had fallen into the river and died of hypothermia.

When someone dies, the Hmong believe that person's soul must return to the original village where he was born. Mourners play a song on the *qeej,* a woodwind made of six bamboo pipes fitted with copper reeds, to guide the spirit over mountains and rivers on this backward journey. The song's duration depends on the age of the deceased and his or her travels through life; it can often take several hours before a dead person's soul finally reaches home. Since the Hmong language is tonal, the musician literally speaks through his instrument, giving directions. So it may not have been coincidence in Fresno when two men dressed in kilts played a dirge for Colby on Scottish bagpipes, the only instrument that rivals the *qeej* for sheer eerieness. The song they played was "Amazing Grace." It's a song of repentance, of course, but an ironic choice under the circumstances, what with its plaintive reference to one who "once was lost, but now am found." Joe Bee, an accomplished *qeej* player, thought the melody appropriately sad but hardly long enough for so extensive an itinerary as a soul might require to find its way home.

A Northern Front

In March of 2003, when the temperature outside was –30° and
falling, I sat in the TV lounge of a construction-camp-turned-hotel
in Kaktovik, a small Inupiat village on an island off Alaska's northeastern corner, staring at the big color console. Villagers checking
for packages from the last mail plane would stomp the snow off
their boots, remove gauntlet mittens, and pull back parka hoods to
look over my shoulder, hoping to catch the girls' state basketball
championship live from Anchorage. What they saw instead was
CNN's telecast of explosions in the desert sky over Baghdad. The
bombing was not unexpected. Still, watching it from an island in
the frozen Beaufort Sea, on the other side of the world, would have
seemed less surreal had events in Iraq not been so publicly connected with where we sat watching them.

Three days before the scheduled invasion of Iraq was to begin,
Senate Republicans had attempted to open the Arctic National
Wildlife Refuge to oil development by attaching a measure to a vote
on a budget resolution, a maneuver designed to avoid a full hear-

ing on an issue Congress has debated for at least twenty years. This time there was a new sense of urgency. Saddam Hussein had played a central role in past arguments to open the Refuge, and this would likely be the last chance to go to that particular well before cruise missiles obviated it altogether. The language of the Senate debate so blurred distinctions between oil reserves in Alaska and those in Iraq that a Democrat urged his colleagues not to "invade this snow desert." There were references to "national security," to "oil as a weapon," even to "the local people [who] are begging us to come in." The "local people" in this case referred to the Inupiat Eskimos of Kaktovik, who favor oil development, rather than to the Gwich'in Indians on the other side of the Brooks Range, who don't. It was necessary that there be "local people" to add a moral dimension to a measure that might otherwise be seen as handing over public land for the profit of a few multinational oil companies. The measure failed by four votes. But nobody in Kaktovik felt this was the end of the matter. If the invasion of Iraq has demonstrated anything, it is that the Bush Administration's fixation on certain issues has remained, well, fixed, even as their rationales have proven flexible and opportunistic.

During the congressional debate, Senator Ted Stevens (R-Alaska) made the coastal plain of the Arctic National Wildlife Refuge sound like the Slough of Despond. When a Democrat held up photographs of wildflowers, he countered with a bleak landscape of white on white. "As far as you can see, nothing but frozen tundra. . . . Ask anybody who's been up there in the wintertime."

So I'd come to see for myself.

My head was swathed like a Bedouin's—balaclava, fleece face mask, yellow-tinted goggles, parka hood—as I drove a clattering snowmobile through the village the day after the bombing of Baghdad began. The snow-banked streets looked milky blue in the early morning light, and a brisk wind had lowered the ambient temperature to −40°. To the windward side of the village, beyond the last modular house, a towering snow fence sixteen feet high—a

Hadrian's Wall of slatted timber—kept Kaktovik from being buried
in drifts.

The coastal plain *is* a desert in terms of precipitation—less than
six inches fall annually—but what falls as snow stays to be later distributed by the wind. Long, hard-packed ridges, or sastrugi, form
in the direction of the prevailing winds, west-east in this case, and
as we headed south across the frozen lagoon to the coastal plain,
the surface was so deeply furrowed that snowmobiling across it felt
like motocross. I was driving a Super Wide Track Ski-Doo that belonged to my Inupiat guide, Robert Thompson. It's designed for
hauling rather than racing, he'd explained, so the suspension was
fairly stiff. When I asked why most of the foam seat was missing,
Robert said that a polar bear had eaten it.

Our plan was to travel southwest across the coastal plain to the
mouth of the Hulahula River and follow its frozen course to the
mountains, a distance of some fifty miles, and set up camp. It is a
journey many Inupiat families make in late spring and fall to hunt
and fish, a trip that in the future may require crossing oil fields and
pipelines.

Two years ago, I'd flown over the coastal plain in early July, the
ocher-colored tundra segmented by ice-wedge polygons and thaw
lakes that mirrored the summer sun. The pilot dipped a wing so I
could see a small band of caribou along a riverbank, scattered gray
dots, each centered over its own shadow. They were the advance
guard of the Porcupine caribou herd on the last leg of an 800-mile
migration to calving grounds. Now the landscape looked utterly
empty, empty and white, and yet winter unlocks the country to
travel in a way impossible in summer. The plain tilts upward almost imperceptibly from the seacoast to the Brooks Range, the
mountains looming to the south like a storm front. It is the abrupt
rise of these mountains, from sea level to almost 8,000 feet, that
accentuates the flatness of the coastal plain. The landscape tends
to magnify anything set against it, and the physical world can be
taken in at a glance—ocean, plain, mountains.

I was careful not to follow Robert too closely because of a twelve-foot wooden sledge he was pulling behind his machine. Heavily loaded with camping gear and extra gas cans, the sledge would occasionally swing wide of the snowmobile's wake in a determined arc until the towrope snapped it back into line. Between the immense snow horizon and the vault of blue sky, there were only these two objects—the snowmobile and the sledge. I couldn't take my eyes off them. To lose sight of them for even a moment meant unmooring myself from all that was human in the landscape, a prospect at once frightening and thrilling.

For some time we had been nearing what looked like the prow of a ship protruding from a snowbank, a prow that seemed always to recede even as we drew closer. It materialized finally as the peaked roof of a small frame house drifted to the window ledges in snow. We went inside to warm up with a thermos of coffee.

The one-room house had been built communally in Kaktovik and hauled to this widening in the river, a place indistinguishable in winter from the surrounding whiteness except that it had a name: First Fish Hole. In another month villagers would come here to fish through the ice for grayling and Arctic char. Some of them had scrawled their names on the wall: Aishanna, Sims, Brower, Akootchook. Robert's wife is an Akootchook, one of the most prominent families in Kaktovik, her father an elder and Presbyterian minister. Robert's background is a little different. His mother was from the village of Wainwright on the Chukchi Sea; his father had come to Alaska by way of Utah. In appearance, Robert favors the Inupiat side of the family, with heavy black eyebrows and a broad, handsome face, but he'd grown up on Lake Minchumina in the interior of Alaska. He traveled a lot, beginning with a tour of Vietnam, where one of his duties was guarding oil tankers in Cameron Bay. He and his wife, Jane, had moved to Kaktovik to raise their family in a village where subsistence hunting and other traditional Native values could be balanced with a cash economy. It is an increasingly difficult balancing act.

"This is where the pipeline would go through," Robert said, looking out the open door. "And there'd be a jetport a few miles from here."

Robert is an outspoken opponent of drilling in the Arctic Refuge, and thus is something of an anomaly in Kaktovik, where nearly every job is connected to oil revenues. Last year, when he and his oldest daughter went to Washington, D.C., with the Alaska Wilderness League to lobby against a bill to open the Refuge, he ran into Senator Stevens, the bill's cosponsor. "So you're here to help us open ANWR," said the senator, when he learned the couple were from Kaktovik. "Actually," Robert told him, "I'm against it."

When Robert and his wife first came back to the village, ice had to be cut in blocks from the freshwater lake west of the village and melted for drinking water; streets were not plowed, and there were few jobs. Now there are water and sewer lines being laid, a new school and health clinic, and the jobs that go with them. Nearly all of this has been paid for by property taxes levied by the North Slope Borough on Prudhoe Bay oil fields. Robert tells a story about his sister-in-law complaining about oil development on the North Slope and the elder Akootchook telling her to try living in a tent and hunting for food if she didn't like progress.

The Arctic National Wildlife Range was established in 1960 when Fred Seaton, the secretary of interior under Eisenhower, signed a public-land order setting aside 8.9 million acres of northeastern Alaska to protect its "unique wildlife, wilderness and recreational values." Twenty years later, Congress passed the Alaska National Interest Lands Conservation Act, renaming the range as a "refuge" and doubling its size, largely to protect the Porcupine caribou herd, but it wavered over 1.5 million acres of the coastal plain between the Canning and Aichilik rivers. Section 1002 of the act called for further study to determine whether the area should be opened to oil and gas development or designated a wilderness. Subsequent studies revealed two things. First, there is a high probability of a

major oil deposit beneath the coastal plain; and second, extracting
that oil and getting it to market pose a significant threat to the environment.

Because there is no easy choice, the public debate over the
disputed land has been waged largely in symbolic language, beginning with what to call the place. Naming, as any explorer knows,
is as much about controlling a landscape as describing it. Pro-
development forces prefer the eponymous "ten-oh-two" in the
same way that they inevitably refer to the Arctic National Wildlife
Refuge as "ANWR," an acronym that manages to sound both vaguely
military and vaguely Middle Eastern. Environmentalists alternate
between the precise "coastal plain" and the overblown "America's
Serengeti." The Inupiat, who were not consulted when the Arctic
Refuge was created, find the term "wilderness" particularly loath-
some, suggesting as it does a place without human habitation or
history. Their own place names, such as First Fish Hole, tend to reflect particular uses people have for the land. A 1985 land-use study
by the Alaska Department of Fish and Game mapped out the subsistence activities of a number of Kaktovik households, the most
extensive of which covered 6,000 square miles, from whaling
grounds off the Beaufort Sea coast to hunting camps secreted deep
within the mountain valleys. Some of the place names within this
vast territory have obvious meanings, such as *Nullaagavik*, which
translates into "place to camp." Other names are more oblique. My
favorite is *Niaquqtuguiqsaagvik*, or "place where the caribou heads
are eaten for the last time," and refers to an area where hunters
lightened their loads by eating the heads of caribou they had killed
in the mountains before returning to the coast.

Somewhere else in this great emptiness is a place called KIC-1,
a test well drilled in 1985 by Chevron and British Petroleum on
land owned by the Kaktovik Inupiat Corporation. The test well has
assumed a mythic quality over the years because it was quickly
capped and the results kept secret. The most recent estimate by the
U.S. Geological Survey suggests that if the price of oil remains at

least $24 a barrel, the 1002 Area could profitably yield about 7 bil-
lion barrels of oil and, at its peak, 4 percent of the United States'
daily requirement, given our current rate of consumption. Even using directional drilling, which requires smaller gravel pads and
leaves a smaller "footprint" upon the land, a number of fields would
be required to extract the oil, since the deposits are so scattered.

Because of the infrastructure needed to move oil to market, an
oil field on the coastal plain would be ugly no matter how small the
"footprint"—the proverbial tarantula on a wedding cake. Then
again, the Inupiat may have a different aesthetic when it comes to
landscape, one that defines beauty in terms of utility. A thing cannot be ugly if it is useful. In such a view, would an oil well be more
obtrusive than the spars of a whaling ship frozen into the lagoon?
Perhaps future generations will look out at a field of nodding der-
ricks and give it a name that fits its use: place where the money
flows out of the ground.

As Robert and I passed the Sadlerochit Mountains, a spur of the
Brooks Range, he spotted a small band of caribou in a swale beyond the riverbank. They were likely wanderers from the Central
Arctic caribou herd rather than the more peripatetic Porcupine
herd. Robert had left his rifle at home on the principle that this was
not strictly a hunting trip and that we'd see more game if he was
unarmed. And, in fact, the caribou continued to paw through the
snow to graze, but I sensed that Robert was having second
thoughts.

Before the Sadlerochit Range, we had crossed an imaginary line
out of the 1002 Area and into designated "wilderness." As the
foothills closed in, there were more willows along the drifted river-
banks and less wind. Ahead lay a white curtain of pyramidal mountains, the tallest of which, Mt. Michelson, dominated the valley with
its sharp, glaciated ridges. We set up camp at Second Fish Hole, a
light-shot bowl of hills just before the river narrows into a canyon.
Springs feed into the river from either side, so there's always an open

lead in the ice. In mid-April, many Kaktovik families set up tents here to hunt and fish, children sliding on the snow hills, teenagers "high-marking" the mountainsides with their snowmobiles.

After the tent was up, Robert went down to the river to fill a pot of water that turned to slush by the time he brought it inside. He set it hissing on the Coleman stove and threw in a freezer bag of caribou stew to thaw. We ate by candlelight, sitting cross-legged on sleeping bags set on a caribou hide. The orange Arctic Oven tent has a special perforated liner that allows it to breathe so that we wouldn't be asphyxiated by propane fumes. All the heat from the stove rose to the peak, but the snow tracked onto the floor never melted.

"If we're going to be against oil development," said Robert, "we have to come up with a sustainable, alternative economy. That's the problem in rural Alaska. There's no economy."

Robert has worked as a heavy-equipment operator and a carpenter, but those jobs kept him away from the land, which was the reason he'd moved his family to Kaktovik in the first place.

"I'd be working on a roof, watching people head out on snowmobiles, and I'd think: There's more to life than money. That's why I got my eco-tourism business going."

Our winter camping trip was an attempt to find a niche market, but he had other ideas—dog-sledding from hut to hut, kayak trips along the barrier islands. At present, tourism in the Refuge is mainly summer rafting trips down North Slope rivers such as the Hulahula. But the ideal tourist season, between ice-out and the onslaught of the Arctic mosquito, is narrow, a month at best. Most of the rafting companies are based outside of Alaska and, according to Robert, "they never, not ever, hire anyone from Kaktovik."

The history of Kaktovik is one of periodic incursions by outsiders, epoch after epoch, each with the bright promise of supplementing the Inupiat's subsistence hunting with a cash economy. The first was Sir John Franklin, who led a party in two open boats down the

Mackenzie River to its mouth and then turned west to map the Beaufort Sea coast. On an August morning in 1826, they spied caribou-skin tents and beached kayaks on a low island, the inhabitants fast asleep. Franklin ordered his Eskimo interpreter to hail them, "and after two or three loud calls, a female appeared in a state of nudity; after a few seconds she called out to her husband, who awoke at the first sound of her voice, and shouting that strangers were close at hand, the whole space between the tents and the water was, in a few minutes, covered with armed, though naked, people."

The Inupiat, who had never seen white people before, were not overly awed. They were travelers themselves, returning from a trading journey to relatives further to the west. Once Franklin's interpreter explained the party's mission, the Inupiat invited the party ashore, but Franklin pressed on, naming things as he went. He named the encampment "Barter Island." (The Inupiat called it *Kaktoavik,* or "place to seine fish.") As the expedition moved westward, Franklin's nomenclature reflected worsening conditions: Foggy Island, Point Anxiety. A month later, pinned down by gales in an ice-bound bay, he reluctantly turned back, but not before naming the expedition's ultima Thule in honor of a fellow naval officer, the first Baron Prudhoe.

Thirty years after Franklin's voyage, whaling ships regularly wintered along the Beaufort Sea coast, their crews supplying the natives with trade goods and contagious diseases. The ships stopped coming once the whales were hunted beyond profitability. The failure of commercial whaling was followed in the 1920s by fur trading and domestic reindeer herding, ventures that ended when the trading post closed and the reindeer either ran off or died. Early in the Cold War, the U.S. Air Force chose Kaktovik for a Distant Early Warning Radar site. The first thing the military did was to bulldoze the old village site and build a runway over it.

Today the economy of Kaktovik and the entire North Slope is based on oil, despite the fact that hardly any Inupiat actually work in the oil fields. In 1974 leaders from the eight Inupiat villages along the Beaufort and Chukchi Sea coasts created the North Slope Borough, geographically the largest municipality in the nation, with fewer than 7,300 residents but with taxing power over the entire Arctic Shelf, including the Prudhoe Bay oil fields. Between 1999 and 2000 the borough collected more than $200 million in property taxes, nearly all of it from a handful of petroleum companies. But as the flow of oil down the Trans-Alaska Pipeline diminishes, so do the tax revenues. That's why most people in Kaktovik support drilling in the Arctic Refuge, even though this time it would be in their own backyard.

The great drawback of winter camping is extricating yourself the next morning from a warm sleeping bag. After waiting as long as possible, I pulled on my boot pacs and ducked behind the tent. In the quiet time I had to study the snow, I recognized the tracks of fox and caribou but not the shambling, manlike prints that angled down from the hillside and through our camp. We were supposedly too far inland for polar bears, and grizzlies normally don't emerge from their dens until mid-April. Nevertheless, Robert looked at the tracks and announced that they belonged to an "early bear": "Early bear is old, has worn-down teeth, and is real hungry."

This was disconcerting news to me since we'd been cooking in the tent and hadn't brought a rifle. Robert was less concerned but went along with my insistence that we at least look for a gun. We hiked up the canyon into the mountains, following another snowmobile trail that the "early bear" had also taken before veering off to the east. The river ice had been heaved up in stretches and made a hollow sound as if we were walking across a drum skin. Later we met a snowmobiler heading in the opposite direction, a rifle slung across his back. When he lifted off his helmet, there were dark brown streaks of frostbite running down his cheeks. He graciously lent us a 7.08mm Mauser with a black plastic stock and a telescopic sight.

"How's the war?" he asked.

"They've stopped dropping leaflets," said Robert, "and started dropping bombs."

Don Burns is a *tunnik*, like myself, though he married a local girl who serves as Kaktovik's assistant mayor. Burns has a long, bony, Appalachian face and punctuates his jokes with a rolling, baritone stage villain's laugh. When Robert brought up drilling in the Refuge, Burns was noncommittal but thought development is inevitable.

"It's like the girl with the best figure in high school and every guy is after her. Every year they keep trying. And eventually you know one of them is going to get lucky."

Then Burns laughed his deep, wicked laugh.

The Inupiat are not the only "local people" with a stake in what becomes of the Arctic Refuge. On the other side of the mountains, along the east fork of the Chandalar River, live the Neets'aii Gwich'in of Arctic Village, the northernmost Indians on the continent. Because salmon do not ascend the river, the Gwich'in depend heavily upon the Porcupine caribou herd, whose migration route leads from the coastal plain to the boreal forests south of the Brooks Range. The Gwich'in worry that oil development on the calving grounds will diminish the herd or cause it to change its migration pattern. Unlike the Inupiat, who had early and repeated contact with whites, the Gwich'in preferred isolation from trading posts and outsiders. Well into the last century, they lived a nomadic existence, following the seasonal movements of game. (A permanent school was not established in Arctic Village until 1959.) In the past, the Gwich'in and Inupiat sometimes crossed the mountains to launch raids on each other's camps or, more often, to trade. Rivers like the Hulahula were natural conduits for such traffic. A Gwich'in shaman and early convert to Christianity named Albert Tritt recorded just such a trading journey made in the winter of 1898.

We made a trip up to Arctic Ocean & bought 3 rifles. . . . That winter, Eskimo came over for first time to our place. Had

*many guns. Killed all kinds of meat. Since then, community
life has disappeared and each for himself is in order. That
year Chief Peter died and things went badly, and each family went his own way.... There has been no real leader of people since then.*

Arctic Village lies at the head of a broad, lake-dotted valley that
terminates in a wall of steeply canted mountains. Compared with
the luminous coastal plain, the forested valley, hemmed in by river
and mountains, can seem dark and foreboding. The current chief
is Evon Peter, whose election at the age of twenty-five marked a
shift in leadership to a generation with as much experience out of
the village as in it. In 2001, the young chief was attending an international conference in Finland when he learned by e-mail that Secretary of Interior Gale Norton planned to visit Arctic Village that
week. The next day Chief Peter caught a flight home. The log-cabin
village is certainly more picturesque than Kaktovik, though poorer.
The 152 permanent residents each earn about $11,000 annually,
half what their Inupiat counterparts make on the other side of the
range. Yet two summers ago, when I flew in to see how the Gwich'in
handled Secretary Norton's visit, the issue on everyone's mind was
not money but caribou.

The meeting was held in the community hall, a large log building decorated for the event with dozens of white sheets of paper
like those Alaska's senator had used to describe the coastal plain,
only instead of being blank these were inked with the heart-shaped
hoofprints of caribou. After greeting Secretary Norton, the young
chief treated her to a brief primer on Alaska Native history, from
the brutal Russian subjugation of the Aleuts in the eighteenth century ("They were put into slavery") to the purchase of Alaska by the
United States in 1867 ("Without the knowledge of our people"). He
reminded the visitors that for purposes of determining citizenship,
the new territorial government had classified Native people into
two categories: civilized and uncivilized. ("To become a citizen, you
couldn't wear skin clothes and you couldn't speak your own Native

language.") He then moved on to the Alaska Native Claims Settlement Act of 1971, widely regarded as the most generous and enlightened piece of legislation in the government's long, dismal record of dealings with indigenous peoples. In all of these events, Evon Peter discerned a common motive—"the wealth of another country"—and it hardly mattered if that wealth took the form of sea-otter pelts or gold or petroleum.

The federal government had long recognized that Alaska's Native people had a unique claim to lands they used and occupied, but put off settling those claims for more than a century. The discovery of a massive oil deposit at Prudhoe Bay in 1968 resulted in a strange convergence of interests that ultimately led to a settlement. The state of Alaska had already begun leasing land to oil companies on the North Slope when then Secretary of Interior Stewart Udall froze all federal land transactions until Native claims were settled. Oil companies needed clear title to begin building the Trans-Alaska Pipeline, and in this Native leaders saw their best opportunity to get their land. The resulting Alaska Native Claims Settlement Act divided 44 million acres and nearly $1 billion among thirteen regional Native corporations and many more village corporations in exchange for their extinguishing all claims based on aboriginal title. But in mandating a corporate structure, the act set up a conflict between traditional practices, such as subsistence hunting and fishing, and corporate boards interested in the bottom line. In southeast Alaska, for example, Native corporations have clear-cut in the Tongass National Forest against the wishes of many of their own tribal members. So Arctic Village, almost alone, had opted out of the settlement act in favor of a reserve run by tribal government. The Gwich'in view efforts to open the Arctic Refuge to oil development as one more instance of outside exploitation of Native resources.

"We want to continue this way of life here," Peter concluded. "We need to protect what we have, and that includes the caribou, and that includes the Arctic National Wildlife Refuge."

After lunch, Secretary Norton, a tall, plain-faced woman with silver-blonde hair, was presented with a hat made from the fur of a white Arctic fox. Then she stood to have her photograph taken in the hat, earflaps akimbo, smiling gamely as if what she was balancing on her head were still a fox. Before beginning her own remarks, she removed the hat.

"We are here today to listen: Each of us from the Interior Department is here to listen to you share your views."

In her subsequent comments, however, the secretary struck a fine balance between asking what the Gwich'in wanted and reminding them that what they wanted hardly mattered to most Americans, who wouldn't know a caribou from a horse and didn't care if they knew.

"We are trying to learn what can be done for all of the citizens of the United States . . . and that means being able to heat homes and have electricity."

Only a few days before her visit, Norton had appointed as her top adviser on Alaskan affairs the former head of Arctic Power, a pro-drilling lobby. The Interior Department's budget that year, as in subsequent years, already assumed revenues from oil and gas-lease sales in the Arctic Refuge. For their part, the Gwich'in understood that the secretary's visit was only a courtesy call, not a fact-finding mission, and that any listening would be symbolic, like wearing a fur hat.

The evening after Gale Norton's plane had flown on to Kaktovik, I ate dinner with Trimble Gilbert, an Episcopal priest who had served as village chief before Evon Peter. It was Trimble's wife who had sewn the white fox hat. Their two-story cabin sits on a hill with a commanding view of the village and the mountains beyond. For supper, Trimble served broiled whitefish that he had netted that morning, along with moose soup, palm-sized pilot bread crackers, and tea. Trimble had given the invocation that began the meeting in Gwich'in, a language so melodious and hushed that the few English words mixed in ("President of the United States and Congress") sounded harsh by comparison. A lantern-jawed man with shoulder-length hair and black-framed glasses, he'd somberly warned Norton about the side effects of development: "I'm not against money. Money is good. You can survive. But if it's too much we're going to lose some people. We buried a lot of nice young people because of drugs and alcohol."

This evening, however, he seemed in high spirits. From the window above the table, he pointed out the cabins where his sons lived and the mountain peaks beyond the timberline. As we ate, he couldn't keep from looking out the window.

"It's beautiful," he said. "Like watching a beautiful video that never stops."

There is no night in the Arctic summer. The sky at midnight is hardly less luminous than at mid-morning. That summer in Arctic Village I was aware that time itself was more fluid, less easily divided into wakefulness and sleep. I was trying to sleep. I had pitched a tent beside the village on a small knoll of sphagnum moss and yellow mountain-avens. I had pulled a stocking cap over my eyes to keep out the light but it couldn't stop the roar of four-wheelers along the one gravel road or, later, someone picking out blues chords on an electric guitar. Billy Gilbert, one of Trimble's sons, was rehearsing his band in the community hall. Sometime before I fell asleep, they played a song by Creedence Clearwater Revival, the notes floating out over the creeks and backwater sloughs, across the silty river to the steeply canted wall of mountains.

> *You don't have to worry 'cause you have no money,*
> *People on the river are happy to give.*
>   *Rolling, rolling, rolling on the river . . .*

The romance of village life is that it's simple. But the two decades following the settlement act saw an epidemic of suicide in Native villages, the collateral effect of alcoholism and despair and young people so marginalized that they come to believe they inhabit nowhere. Years ago, in a village on the Yukon, I'd watched the body of a suicide being borne up from the beach in a tarp. Who knows why he killed himself? A study of seven Athabascan villages along the Yukon and Koyukuk rivers in the 1980s found that the suicide rate among young Native males was forty times the national average. The study's author described the complex of causes in terms of a house fire: "The winds are powerful forces historical and current, distant and local . . . government policies that lead to local loss of control over subsistence resources, sexual abuse as a child, create tinder-dry houses. The gasoline spilled on them is alcohol . . . the spark is loss of a girlfriend or other immediate stressor."

Despite their divergent paths, the Gwich'in and Inupiat surely want the same thing, which is to feel at home in the world on their own terms. No matter how the debate over the Arctic Refuge is cast elsewhere, in the villages it is fundamentally a question of how one balances a cash economy tied to the outside with a hunting culture irrevocably connected to the land. Students at the Inupiat's Harold Kaveolook Middle School recently put together a booklet in which they asked village leaders what they imagined Kaktovik would be like in another fifty years. The president of the Kaktovik Inupiat Corporation thought that "the village might be bigger, with more houses and people . . . [and] that his grandchildren's homes will be heated with natural gas." A surprising number of city officials predicted that Kaktovik would be underwater as a result of global warming melting the Arctic ice pack. A new teacher from outside suggested that the village would "still be culturally rich," but this sentimental view was undercut by a resident teacher's aide who advised the students to "go see what's in the world for you and don't get stuck in Kaktovik."

Only on a map does any place seem like the end of the earth. Soon enough it becomes here, the focal point of time present, the epicenter of the world. On the last night Robert Thompson and I camped beside the mountains at Second Fish Hole, the Arctic Oven tent had begun to seem mysteriously homelike, and I'd for-

gotten all about "early bears." Before turning in, I went outside to
monogram the snow and happened to glance up. Pale green light
wavered in ghostly columns across the star-tracked sky. How lucky,
I thought, to be here, in this quiet place, and to have escaped the
inevitable noise of war.

On our way home, Robert spotted the same band of caribou in
the saddle of a ridge. They were less than a mile away, and I had
failed even to notice them. We stopped behind a snowbank so that
Robert could unhitch the sled; then he started off toward them, always keeping a ridgeline between himself and the band. After a
while, I climbed the snowbank and scanned the foothills with
binoculars. I could no longer see the band, only two infinitesimally
small dark figures moving against the vast white landscape. I didn't
hear the shot from the borrowed Mauser, but saw the smaller figure pause even as the other stumbled away from it.

The carcass of the young bull caribou raised a small wake as
Robert dragged it behind his snowmobile. He removed his gauntlet mittens and set to work skinning the caribou before it froze
solid. Slipping the knife blade under the thick belly fur just above
the testicles, he slit the hide upward to the sternum so he could tip
out the insides and separate the heart, liver, and kidneys from the
steaming gut pile. Then he peeled away the hide from the body, beginning at the neck and working downward, as if helping the animal out of a tight-fitting jacket. Attached to the underside of the
skin were grape-sized larvae of the botfly. Robert held one out on
the tip of his knife.

"Want to try one? Old people say they taste like milk."

When I declined, Robert admitted he'd never eaten one either.
But he did slice up a kidney, which we ate raw. The meat tasted like
warm blood. Then he quartered the caribou, cut off its head, and
wrapped the parts in the hide for the trip back. We left behind an
appalling amount of blood congealing on the snow, but given the
current state of affairs in the world it hardly seemed tragic.

Before reaching First Fish Hole, we left the river and headed

across the coastal plain to avoid the rough surface of the frozen
Beaufort Sea. By late afternoon, with the sun falling toward the
horizon, the snow turned a shade of apricot. The horizontal plain
was unbroken except for a dome-shaped pingo formed by permafrost and the ever-present sastrugi. Testifying before a House committee last March, Gale Norton described the coastal plain as if the
landscape were trying to escape its fate disguised as scenery. "There
are no trees, there are no deepwater lakes. There are no mountains.
. . . This is what I saw when I was there. . . . This image of flat, white
nothingness." She was describing the view from an airplane, forehead pressed against the window, a downward perspective from
which any landscape looks flattened. She evidently had forgotten
what the tundra had looked like when she flew over it two summers
before. She must have been unfamiliar with Wallace Stevens's
poem "The Snow Man," with its distinction between the "Nothing
that is not there and the nothing that is."

Perhaps we have lost the language to describe a landscape beyond the terminology of real estate brokers: *No trees, no deepwater
lakes, no mountains.* In the late eighteenth century, when philoso-
phers attempted to categorize realms of human experience with the
same precision scientists would later apply to natural species, they
established a clear hierarchy between the merely Beautiful and the
Sublime. The latter provoked an intensity of emotion that Im-
manuel Kant defines as "tranquillity tinged with terror." These
days, the word "sublime" is a joke, the province of old drawing-
room comedies, a parody of itself, and yet what I felt on the coastal
plain was unmistakably "tranquillity tinged with terror." The Inupiat have their own word for such mixed emotions: *uniari,* or
"nervous awe" in the face of overpowering Nature. It is the original
shock and awe.

Ahead, across the frozen lagoon, we could see Barter Island and the
nest of telephone poles and electric wires at one end that marks
Kaktovik. The Thompsons live at the end of a drifted street in a

comfortable modular home leased from the North Slope Borough. After a delicious caribou roast that Jane fixed for dinner, we sat in a living room piled high with stacks of newsletters, magazines, and videos, most relating to "The Cause," as Robert calls it. On the bookshelves: *Alaska Natives and American Laws, In the Wake of* Exxon Valdez, *Ancient People of the Arctic, Black's Law Dictionary, Argumentation and Debate*. Robert ran a video that began with aerial shots of the Hulahula River in summer, braided channels pulsing across the green coastal plain. Then we watched a sixty-second Atlantic Richfield Company advertisement filmed in Kaktovik with an Inupiat elder as its narrator. It was not immediately clear what the ad was trying to sell or to whom. "I've seen a lifetime of progress," said the old man, "and much of it can be good." The camera cut to an oil facility at Prudhoe Bay. "These are our neighbors."

Robert sighed. It can't be easy being the only contrarian in the village.

Later that night we walked to the community hall to hear a delegation from ExxonMobil make a presentation on a proposed development at Point Thomson on the western boundary of the Arctic Refuge. We helped ourselves to platters of smoked halibut and salmon, florets of fresh shrimp, fresh fruit, and an enormous chocolate cake shaped like a whale. The event was a reenactment in microcosm of initial contacts between aboriginals and Westerners: There was the feast; there were gifts—imitation Leatherman tools inscribed with "Point Thomson Project" on one side and "ExxonMobil" on the other—and there was a pitch.

The Point Thomson Project (since postponed) had called for thirteen wells to be drilled from two onshore pads to extract gas condensate and pump it twenty-two miles to a larger, preexisting pipeline. In addition, construction would include a central processing facility, a 100-bed dormitory, a utility module, an airstrip, a barge dock, a dredged channel to the dock, a gravel mine, and an all-weather road to connect the parts.

Balancing a paper plate of food, Robert inspected a large

photograph on the wall that showed caribou crossing a gravel road beside a section of elevated pipe. Spotting Robert's interest, a young ExxonMobil employee from Houston showed him a piece of steel pipe that he said was impervious to bullets. Having arranged a smile on his face, he appeared uncomfortable in the role of salesman.

"You can still hunt caribou."

"Who wants to hunt in a place like that?" said Robert. "It's not very nice, is it?"

"No. It isn't," the young Texan admitted, looking crestfallen because he'd been told the locals were friendlies. "I'm just a plumber. I just put in the pipe."

Robert next inserted himself into a discussion with a bearded man in a plaid shirt who was explaining to some villagers how ExxonMobil avoided disturbing polar bears by flying over suspected den sites with an infrared camera to see if they were occupied. Robert piped in that he'd seen snowmobile tracks over a den site near Flaxman Island.

"It wasn't ours."

"Whose else could it have been?" Robert replied, in his smiling, persistent, infuriating way.

Since the initial discovery of oil at Prudhoe Bay, industrial development has sprawled across the North Slope, yet by focusing on each new project separately—the size of its particular "footprint" and threat to specific wildlife populations—we've lost sight of the cumulative effects of thirty years of oil development on the Arctic Shelf. Technology may have shrunk the size of drilling pads, but there are more of them, and they are all linked. Currently, there are twenty-four active oil fields connected by 600 miles of roads and permanent trails. And this is just the beginning. The U.S. Geological Survey estimates reserves of 9.3 billion barrels of oil in the massive National Petroleum Reserve to the west of Prudhoe Bay, more than in the 1002 Area, though less lucrative to extract.

With 95 percent of the North Slope open to oil and gas leasing, the mystery is why people in Kaktovik would allow their backyard to be converted into an industrial complex given that they currently have the best of both worlds—oil revenues and unrestricted access to hunting and fishing grounds. The same cannot be said of the village of Nuiqsut, on the Colville River, whose mayor recently testified at a public hearing on the effects of oil-field sprawl: "Once upon a time I lived in a community where subsistence game was abundant and social impact was virtually invisible. Today I am practically surrounded by steel oil pipelines, ice roads, exploration equipment, development plants, and drilling rigs. I continue to deal with the impacts on a daily basis."

Nuiqsut is the village of the future.

By the time I got back to my hotel, the ExxonMobil men were sitting at the dining-room table, their photographs and schematic diagrams of Point Thomson (what one of them called "our show-and-tell") leaning against the wall. Aside from the plumber from Houston, they were a well-traveled group; one had worked the year before in Saudi Arabia, another on Sakhalin Island off the Pacific coast of Russia. The oil business is global, a merchant empire in itself.

The men seemed in a merry mood, but when I poured a cup of coffee and sat down, they all stood up and left. To look at the northern lights, they said. I finished my coffee and went into the TV lounge to catch up on the war news. CNN showed columns of black smoke pouring from a burning oil field in Basra. A few minutes later, the ExxonMobil party returned, stamping their boots and smiling as if they'd seen something. I asked how the aurora borealis had looked.

"It was beautiful," one of them said.

The Appraisal

In 1931, a year after *American Gothic* made his reputation, Grant
Wood painted another rural allegory called *Appraisal*. As in the
more famous painting, a backdrop of clapboard porches and out-
buildings leads into two figures in the foreground: one is a farm
woman, the other is her city counterpart, and between them is a
Plymouth Rock hen—the object of their meeting. Although *American Gothic* had annoyed his rural neighbors by offering them up to
patrons of the Art Institute of Chicago as repressed yokels, Wood's
next painting turned the tables. He entered *Appraisal* in a competition at the Iowa Fair, where—no surprise—it won. Fairgoers in
the summer of 1931 were just beginning to see corn and hog prices
free-fall; around the corner lay sheriff's sales, penny auctions, and
martial law. How satisfying then to step from the stink of livestock
barns into the art pavilion and see the city represented as a fat lady.
Distrust between city and country predates the Great Depression,
of course, and persists today in a thousand achy ballads in which
thrift and physical labor go unrewarded while some lazy slick-ass

reaps the benefits. This is the theme of Wood's painting, and its central metaphor is consumption. The city woman, rich and useless, is so busy appraising the chicken that she's oblivious to being appraised herself. The farm woman, on the other hand, is virtue and hard work personified. Keeping a firm grip on the chicken, she manages the thinnest of smiles, but her sidelong glance is wary and alert, as if this city visitor were one more in a long line of scheming two-faced sharpies.

Grant Wood, Appraisal, *oil, 1931.*
Courtesy of the Carnegie-Stout Public Library, Dubuque, Iowa.

In October 1998, Kathy King was combining a ten-acre soybean field above her farmhouse in southeastern Minnesota. Even from a distance, anyone could tell who was at the helm of the John Deere 9400: "Kathy" was painted in yellow on the side, because, as her husband, Terry, likes to point out, the combine had cost as much as a yacht. From its elevated cab, Kathy could look out on four townships: Section One of Rock Dell, which the King farm occupies, and the corners of three others. It was a bird's-eye perspective on a landscape of almost pure geometric proportions, a landscape redrawn by machines every autumn as combines level the buff-colored fields, followed by chisel plows working in from the edges until black dirt frames the bare rectangles and the countryside resembles nothing so much as a plat map of itself. But Kathy's gaze was focused a few feet beyond the header as it mowed a swath through the tangle of soybeans. Her eyes, blue and alert behind steel-rim glasses, worked overtime looking for chunks of limestone that can float to the surface from one season to the next, especially in this tilting, comma-shaped field.

Kathy had learned to combine on this very field twenty years earlier under conditions of some urgency. That harvest season had begun in a cold rain. After four rounds, Terry had parked the combine to cut firewood in the woodlot below the house. Kathy was in the kitchen when she heard their oldest boy, then eleven, gun the small utility tractor into the yard. She was about to reprimand him for hot-rodding when the boy ran inside and sobbed that there'd been an accident. A big elm had bucked backward and caught Terry in the chest. Both the ambulance and sheriff's deputy who arrived had to be towed out of the mud by tractor before Terry could be taken the ten miles to Saint Mary's Hospital in Rochester. While he recuperated, with broken ribs and a bruised heart, his wife resumed the harvest. Although she'd grown up on a farm, Kathy had never driven anything as big as the 9400's predecessor. The ten-acre field was still greasy from the rains when she began, but she managed to keep the combine erect and moving. She did not real-

ize, amid the muffled ping of beans filling the hopper, that a bolt
had fallen into the reel until the entire header collapsed, sickle
blades flying, and the combine lurched to a halt. A local implement
dealer lent her a new header, and a neighbor in his seventies vol-
unteered to help while his wife baby-sat the King children. He'd
show up about nine in the morning, and together they would
grease up machinery and shuttle grain wagons until the dew was
off, then combine long into the night, walking back to the farmhouse in its circle of arc light and the pinholes in the darkness beyond that constituted their neighborhood.

This October the weather was holding dry, the harvest on schedule, when Kathy got a phone call at lunch from her neighbor Bill
Kuisle. From her front window she could see the Kuisles' silo across
the valley on Yankee Ridge. "Are you sitting down, Kathy?"

"Yes." She laughed and waited for the other shoe to drop.

"Did you know you're getting a railroad?"

Kuisle, a state representative, sat on the steering committee of a
city-county task force studying a proposal by the Dakota, Minnesota & Eastern Railroad to upgrade its track through Rochester.
The upgrade was a small part of a $1.5 billion project to extend the
rail line into Wyoming's Powder River Basin from its eastern ter-
minus on the Mississippi River. The DM&E expansion, the largest
railroad project proposed in a century, would carry low-sulfur coal
to eastern utilities facing more stringent air-quality controls. The
steering committee, however, was considering moving the railroad
out of Rochester and into the countryside. Kuisle had seen a map
of the proposed bypass. The tracks would bisect the King farm just
above the house, taking out a new pole shed and five grain bins,
and exiting through the ten-acre field.

Two landmarks dominate the skyline of Rochester, Minnesota. One
is the fourteen-story brick-and-terra-cotta Plummer Building, flag-
ship of the world-famous Mayo Clinic; the other is the old Libby
canning plant's green-and-yellow water tower, shaped like a giant

ear of corn. Together they represent the city's past and future. So many parks and schools and public buildings are named after the Mayo brothers, Drs. Will and Charlie, that the two could be mistaken for Rochester's mythic twins, their origins intertwined with the city's own. The town was founded on wheat, but sick people made it rich. Today, Rochester is a city of hotel rooms and florist shops and a shifting population of "visitors," some dressed strangely for the Midwest in kaffiyehs and flowing robes, some with entourages and bodyguards—all of them pilgrims of a sort. Ranking Rochester at the top of its list of Best Small Cities in America, *Money* magazine noted that it possessed "the sophistication of a larger metro area, but not the congestion or the complications. There are several art galleries, good restaurants and a repertory theater." But when one overhears the visitors in the good restaurants, the talk is pointedly not of art galleries or repertory theater but of invasive procedures and long-term prognoses, and the "congestion" and "complications" to be avoided are chiefly the result of secondary infection. So merged is the town's identity with its largest employer that the 1.5 million visitors cited by the Chamber of Commerce is exactly equal to the number of outpatient visits to the Clinic. In a literal sense, the Mayo Clinic is downtown Rochester, now occupying 10 million square feet (two and a half times the floor space of the Mall of America). And if the Clinic required a railroad bypass, then so did the city, which understands only too well the source of its many visitors, its flower shops and hotels, its "unexpected" sophistication, because to imagine Rochester without Mayo would be to imagine another middling prairie town, one more hicksville with a water tower shaped like a giant ear of corn.

A week after Bill Kuisle's phone call to Kathy King, six hundred mostly rural residents of Olmsted County crowded into the Mayo Civic Center in a bad mood. They were angry because they'd received a letter from Kuisle informing them that the steering committee was about to issue a final recommendation regarding a bypass through their land. I was there because my in-laws had received one of those letters. Our collective mood worsened as we read an addendum to the task force's agenda: "NOTE TO INTERESTED CITIZENS—There will be NO public hearing this evening."

"We would like to caution everyone from making assumptions or jumping to conclusions regarding any of the options recommended as solutions," said cochair Dave Bishop, a state legislator from Rochester and owner of Bishop Properties.

"This divisive issue is not caused by any of the citizens of Olmsted County nor by any of our local government units," the white-haired Bishop continued. His cranky demeanor and orotund delivery suggested Lionel Barrymore giving the riffraff of Bedford Falls a good tongue-lashing. "It is caused by a proposal from a railroad that wishes to profit by shipping a commodity, coal, through our County. . . . If you are concerned about the trains, lay that responsibility on the DM&E railroad. This is a difficult issue for all of us."

We all booed.

The crowd understood perfectly well that the city and the Mayo Clinic, not the railroad, wanted to move the tracks into the countryside. For the past week, the city had run TV spots predicting forty coal trains a day roaring through town unless a bypass was built (a figure the DM&E disputes).* Classrooms of city schoolchildren wrote letters to the Surface Transportation Board, the federal agency that regulates rail transit, some illustrated with drawings of killer locomotives run amok on city streets. Monthly utility bills included flyers urging residents to inform the STB that coal trains were not welcome in Rochester. Nobody mentioned that the only coal currently hauled by the DM&E Railroad supplies Rochester Public Utilities.

---

* The DM&E estimates that even if it ran an optimum thirty-four trains per day on its entire system, only ten would reach Rochester; the rest would be rerouted at interchanges west of the city.

The floor was soon given over to a short, balding consultant with the heroic name of Leif Thorson. Thorson's engineering firm had been hired by the task force to study the DM&E's proposed upgrade of its tracks through Rochester as well as alternatives, including a rural bypass.

"Now we're going to look at the Decision Matrix," he announced, projecting an overhead transparency divided into multiple columns. "A matrix is a list of issues and options. It's a vehicle for comparing, if you will."

Some of the options were purely fanciful—a trench through the city, a tunnel—and the consultant whittled away at these until only two remained that weren't, in his words, "fatally flawed": DM&E's proposal to upgrade its existing tracks through Rochester or the city's plan to build a thirty-six-mile bypass south through the countryside. On the surface, the choice seemed self-evident. The existing route was shorter, straight as an arrow, traversed minimum grade, and, most significantly, was already there. The bypass, on the other hand, was circuitous, redundant (since the existing route would remain to serve the city's own energy needs), and cost taxpayers anywhere from $100 to $300 million. Hence the need for consultants. And Thorson compared the bypass not with the railroad's own proposed upgrade through town but with an "enhanced" version prepared by his firm: although the DM&E proposal displaced no homes or businesses (since it used the existing trackbed), the "enhanced" version uprooted fourteen businesses and sixty-nine homes, nearly doubling the cost. Thorson worked the opposite magic with the bypass, shrinking its costs by, essentially, making the rural population disappear.

"Displacement of households," said Thorson, moving his finger along the matrix's bypass column, "ten to fifteen. Displacement of businesses . . . none."

"What about farms?" a voice shouted. "Isn't a farm a business?"

"Well," said the consultant, perplexed by the question, "we didn't consider farms as businesses."

Hoots and catcalls.

The bypass route traversed fifty-odd farms, and even if trains didn't smash through the farmhouse the result was likely to be the same. Yet this point was difficult to get across because the audience wasn't allowed to address the meeting except to ask questions. Here are the questions I should have asked: If a farm isn't a business, then what is it? And if you divert a railroad through a farm so that the farmer cannot get to his crops and his livestock cannot get to pasture or water, don't you put him out of business? And if you put him out of business, don't you also put him out of his home?

But I sat on my hands.

"Minnesota Nice" is a phrase often invoked by state politicians when doling out bad news. The polite silence that follows isn't modesty or reserve but a variety of fatalism, the self-defeating conviction that you're going to get screwed anyway so you might as well take it quietly instead of making a public spectacle of yourself. It is part of a rural ethos, an ethos in which language, or an excess of language, is always suspect, the sure sign of a bullshitter. It explains, in part, why American farmers are so reluctant to protest even as they're relentlessly edged out of the market, preferring to go down quietly with the ship, one ship at a time.

Someone asked Thorson why the Decision Matrix had no figures on rural road closings or resulting delays in emergency-response time in the country, where it always takes longer for the ambulance to arrive. The consultant did not have an answer. He scanned the crowd, looking for a friendly face, someone in a coat and tie, someone like me. "Okay," he said affably. "Does anyone have figures on rural roads?" "Shouldn't you?" I yelled. "You're the consultant!"

On October 8, 1864, the *Rochester City Post* carried the following editorial:

> *Jubilate! Jubilate! — That is what everybody and his Wife ejaculated on hearing last week for the first time in Rochester*

the whistle of the locomotive. . . . bless our stars that we live in
the days of Railroads, and that it is our good fortune to dwell
in a section of country traversed thereby. . . . [A]ll hail to the
welcome blasts of the shrill whistles which break from the
iron throats of monster locomotives.

Railroads were the arbiters of destiny in nineteenth-century America, vanquishing both time and space, and their arrival secured Rochester's future. Farmers had a more complicated relationship with the railroad. In the 1870s, when the railroad doubled its freight rates, a vocal critic was Rochester's horse-and-buggy practitioner, Dr. William Worrall Mayo. A farmer by preference, he was elected to the state legislature on the populist Farmer's Alliance ticket. "If I could treat this railroad company in my profession," he declared, "I would give them such a puke as would bring their corns from their toes through their stomachs." His sons, Doctors Will and Charlie, however, recognized the railroad's importance to the growth of their small-town clinic, and by the 1930s an express train equipped with special cars transported patients from Chicago to Rochester. By then the railroad was no longer the big dog in town; the Clinic was.

The day after Christmas, my father-in-law received a letter from Rochester mayor Chuck Canfield. Although his jurisdiction does not extend to my family's land in Marion Township, the mayor had assumed responsibility for informing my in-laws that their farm lay within 1,200 feet of a potential railroad corridor (in fact the bypass would cut the place in half) as well as detailing the means by which their land could be taken. "This would require an appraisal of the property to determine the value, with an opportunity for a separate appraisal by the property-owner. These appraisals form the basis for a negotiated settlement."

But how is my father-in-law to appraise the farm he grew up on, that belonged to his father and grandfather, a place he never left except to fly P-38s in the Pacific? This corner of Marion Township was settled by Irish immigrants, many of whom came west with the railroad and settled on quarter-sections of rolling upland that reminded them of County Wexford or Cork. The surnames on the current township plat—Sheehan, Touhey, Griffin, O'Neill—are those inscribed in the lancet windows of St. Bridget's Church and on the white headstones in the adjoining cemetery. My in-laws were being asked to give up not just acreage but their stake in a neighborhood older and more tightly woven than any elm-shaded cul-de-sac in Rochester.

A memo attached to the mayor's letter reminded my in-laws of the town's big dog. "Finally, the main foundation for the employment base for the City of Rochester and for this entire area is based on the services provided by the Mayo Clinic and their ability to compete with health care providers in quality communities throughout the State, the United States, and internationally. There are alternative locations for health care that could be chosen by a percentage of the Mayo Clinic patients. We want to ensure that they continue to choose Rochester."

In Minnesota, rural schoolhouses that haven't been torn down or converted to grain bins enjoy a second life as township halls. The township is the six-mile square division that served as Thomas Jefferson's blueprint for an agrarian republic, a vision that never quite got off the drawing board, its vestigial outlines still visible in ruler-straight roads that run in cardinal directions, spaced exactly a mile apart. Although township government survives in the Midwest and New England, its political powers were largely absorbed by the county after reapportionment in the 1960s, which based representation on population size. In rural areas, like most of Olmsted County, overshadowed by a single midsize city, the township remains the most intimate form of government. Apart from maintaining roads and levying property taxes, the township provides a sounding board that, in de Tocqueville's words, can still "excite the warmest of human affections without arousing the ambitious passions of the heart of man."

Salem Town Hall, a prairie-style former schoolhouse, stands at a crossroads opposite a trailer park and the Hiawatha Valley Farm Store. On a cold evening in December, my brother-in-law, Steve Raduenz, and I left his car parked beside a snowbank and hurried inside, where it was warmer but not much. People stood around in coats and hats until someone adjusted the thermostat and the heat kicked in. A pennant on the wall read "Salem Sailors 4-H Club— Helping Kids Sail into the 21st Century." But everything about the place seemed stuck in the past: the cream-colored wainscoting and old wooden floor, the optimistic 4-H banners, even the audience, some of whom must have attended school here.

Dressed in a loden blazer and gray turtleneck, Kathy King looked like the schoolteacher she used to be. "We are waiting," she said, "for the lawyer to arrive." In short order, she brought us up to speed on the newly formed Citizens Against the Bypass. In the three weeks since the task force meeting in Rochester, the group had collected hundreds of names on a petition, written the county's eighteen townships as well as state and federal legislators, and invited an attorney (en route) to explain our situation. In almost every instance, she'd found the Mayo Clinic about eight months ahead in terms of lining up political support.

The lawyer, a large-boned woman in owlish glasses, arrived in a cloud of frost. She had spent the afternoon arguing a right-of-way case on the other side of the state, and now, catching her breath, she explained that the fate of a bypass around Rochester was in the hands of the Surface Transportation Board, which would prepare an environmental impact statement for the entire DM&E proposal. If the STB could be persuaded to exclude the bypass, then we'd be home free. But it would mean a long uphill battle with the city, not to mention the great and powerful Mayo Clinic. That said, she announced that her fee would be $170 an hour with a retainer of $5,000.

Kathy suggested asking for a donation of $300 per family along the bypass route. "What do you think? Should we go ahead?"

The vote was unanimous.

When we took a break, a man in a nylon jacket brought back two Cokes from the store across the street and presented one to the attorney: "Down payment."

On the night of a public forum on the bypass, Kathy King went to the barn to feed her horses. She planned to finish chores, then drive to the Mayo Civic Center in time for the forum. But as she doled out hay and oats, she noticed that one of the horses, a twenty-year-old bay, was strangely agitated, kicking the stall and grinding its teeth. Caught between the demands of civics and animal husbandry, she called the vet. After he tubed the sick horse— squeezing mineral oil and antibiotics down its throat—Kathy spent the evening walking the horse around until its breathing seemed normal. She got back to the house in time to turn on the ten o'clock news. What she saw was me, barking at a television reporter and looking strangely agitated.

Instead of the promised open forum, the steering committee had substituted a consensus-building format called the Chadwick Process. The audience was divided into small "consensus groups" overseen by a trained "facilitator" who elicited comments, then codified them under uniform headings to be later digested privately by the steering committee. In short, the Chadwick Process was a kind of Waring blender in which specific arguments could be whipped into harmless fluff. If you complained, for example, that a bypass would separate your cows from their water source, the facilitator might write: "Coal trains cause economic worries." This is what caused the uproar.

"Remember," said Paul Wilson, cochair of the steering committee and head designer for Whiting's Flowers and Greenhouse. "To participate in the small-group process, you must be seated."

Shouting over Wilson, I insisted that we'd been promised a pub-

lic forum, and this surely wasn't it. As a compromise, the task force
allowed two minutes of open microphone at the end. About twenty
people took their turn, and none of them raised their voice. Most
complained that the makeup of the steering committee unfairly favored the city. The last to speak was my father-in-law's veterinarian, Doc Predmore, a laconic man I've never seen in anything but
faded overalls and a field cap with a Special Forces pin in the
crown. Tonight was no exception.

"What about it, Paul? Could we get more rural representation
on the steering committee?"

Wilson, a florist in a spot, said he'd look into it.

A few weeks later, Wilson called Kathy King to ask if she'd join
the steering committee. At the first meeting, the county attorney
waxed eloquent on his recent trip to the western part of the
DM&E's proposed expansion, and lamented the damage the railroad would inflict on the hardworking ranchers and "pristine
landscape" there. When Kathy pointed out that a bypass around
Rochester threatened farmland every bit as beautiful as ranches
in the colorful West, the attorney looked at the table. Nobody said
anything.

Citizens Against the Bypass was apparently making an impact. A
Mayo Clinic memo entitled "DM&E Railroad—Communications
Strategy" acknowledged that "the public comment period comes at
a time when bypass opponents have mobilized public opinion in
their favor" and outlined several steps to reverse this setback, including the following:

"Deemphasize and do not reference the bypass in public communication, instead focus energy on the damaging effects of the
proposal . . .

"Mobilize business and civic leaders and public opinion, en-
couraging them to contact their federal elected officials or members of the Surface Transportation Board."

The memo described the proposed upgrade through Rochester

as a threat on the order of a nuclear disaster. But much of the perceived threat was to the Clinic's own financial well-being.

"Any modest decrease in patient volumes would have a significant negative impact on Mayo's financial performance. Thus any deterioration in our environment that causes patients not to come to Rochester, threatens both Mayo's and the region's economy."

More to the point, Dr. Michael Murray, chairman of Mayo's public affairs committee, told the local newspaper that "increased rail traffic . . . could slow or halt clinic growth."

It's absurd to think of ailing sheikhs, or anyone, choosing health care on the basis of train traffic. Patients come to Rochester because Mayo is a brand name, with a product recognition based in part on the Clinic's marketing of its bucolic setting. Ironically, a bypass would destroy exactly those environs that make Rochester such a "pleasant, clean, peaceful community." For one thing, the rural townships provide the Clinic with a steady source of inexpensive and reliably "nice" workers. And who's to say that a patient facing the next round of chemo wouldn't prefer to contemplate cornfields and pastures rather than his own ticking clock?

The death of the family farm is the longest-running melodrama in the nation's repertoire, its first act begun after the Civil War, when the number of Americans living on farms first fell below the number who didn't. Today, fewer than 2 percent live on farms. In the last decade alone, the number of farmers in Minnesota and Iowa has declined by 25 percent. And when the last one goes, why should we care? There's not much chance we'll go hungry, and the "farmer" will endure as an advertising icon, a plaid-shirted geezer who needs a jolt of coffee or a bowl of high-fiber cereal before mounting an antique tractor and thundering into the sunrise. In the end, what we'll have lost will be those last reminders of who we once were as a nation and sometimes still pretend to be.

By early summer the rolling cropland of Olmsted County makes you wonder if Grant Wood wasn't a photorealist instead of a painter whose dreamy farmscapes seem pumped with estrogen. His landscapes are always feminine, not hilly fields but breasts and buttocks in which the farmer sinks his plow. The subtext is not sex but fecundity. The earth yields up her bounty season after season, asking nothing in return but the best years of your life.

I'd come down to help my father-in-law separate his calves, so he could inoculate them and castrate the young bulls. But when I arrived, the separating was over, the calves bunched in a small corral beside the barn and a fence behind which the cows kept up a terrible bawling. The ones with yellow plastic ear tags belonged to a cousin, Dennis O'Neill, who'd been renting the cropland and soon would take over all of the pasture. At seventy-nine, my father-in-law was calling it quits after this year—his last roundup, as it were.

Dennis did the vaccinating while his two teenage sons brought calves up from the small corral one at a time and into the squeeze chute. The first calf was a small brown heifer with long-lashed rabbit eyes. Once the calf was immobilized in a head clamp, Dennis shot a pistol-grip syringe into its neck and released the clamp.

"Watch this one," my father-in-law said. "He's frisky."

The bull calf promptly kicked Dennis in the leg. Hobbling after the calf into the chute, Dennis inoculated him, then knelt down and used a spreader to slip two small rubber bands over the calf's balls that would cause the testes to eventually atrophy and fall off. Released, the newly made steer stepped gingerly into the cow yard, uncertain of the damage done.

Nobody mentioned the railroad bypass, though just by looking up we could see where it would go, just east of the barn, on the level cropland, cutting the farm in half. There were more immediate problems at hand. Dennis had just bailed out of the hog business after the market dropped to eleven cents a pound, not enough to cover feed costs, let alone labor, which in Dennis's case included the efforts of his sons. Sean, the youngest, was all smirk and wisecrack to his older brother's gravitas. Dennis rode them equally hard.

"Get off your ass, boys, and see if you can't do two things at once!"

Pat, seventeen, looked like every teacher's nightmare—Marine haircut, cutoff T-shirt, engineer boots, Harley Davidson cap—except that he carried himself with more dignity than any teenager I know and was certainly harder working. He'd spent the summer driving heavy machinery for a construction company but planned to farm like his father. I didn't know whether to admire his determination or run the kid through the squeeze chute and beat some sense into him.

For an entire week, the *Rochester Post-Bulletin* donated full-page ads outlining the horrors of coal trains. The city was about to be pillaged by the Dakota, Minnesota & Eastern Railroad and its ruthless CEO, Kevin Schieffer, the reincarnation of every empire-building robber baron since railroad magnate James J. Hill.

"This Schieffer is not a nice guy," a baggy-pants environmentalist told an audience at Episcopal Church on the city's north side. "This guy is thinking of lining his own pockets. Money! Money! Money!" The speaker whapped the screen with a stick whenever Schieffer's grinning face appeared. "Is he going to stop for a wheelchair on the tracks? No! So who's in favor of the railroad? Schieffer, Schieffer, and Schieffer. Money! Money! Money!"

When Kathy King invited Schieffer to a question-and-answer session at an American Legion hall south of Rochester, the railroad baron agreed. At forty-two, he looked fit and boyish in an open-neck sport shirt and matching slacks. Describing himself as "a recovering attorney," he told the rural crowd what they most wanted to hear.

"We have no interest in building a bypass around Rochester. I think there's no need to build a bypass around Rochester. Before you even get into the cost issues or engineering feasibility issues or the operational issues or the safety issues or anything else, the fundamental question is this: will this thing solve more problems than it creates? The answer is no."

Schieffer was two years out of law school when he became a legislative aide to a South Dakota senator fighting to keep the Chicago and North Western Railway from abandoning its lines through his state. In 1986 a group of investors purchased 900 miles of track to form the DM&E, but some sections of track were so old that trains could only operate at ten miles an hour, and even then averaged half a dozen derailments a month. One train derailed while standing still when the century-old track buckled beneath it.

The DM&E currently hauls mainly bentonite clay from western South Dakota, kaolin clay from Minnesota, forest products out of the Black Hills, and cement from Rapid City, as well as grain, which makes up 40 percent of its business. But Schieffer was pinning the railroad's future on coal. As of last year, the federal Clean Air Act requires utilities to use cleaner-burning coal such as the low-sulfur coal mined in Wyoming's Powder River Basin. By upgrading its current tracks and building 280 miles of new track into Wyoming, DM&E could cut 30 percent off the distance its competitors, Union Pacific and Burlington Northern Santa Fe, now travel to haul the low-sulfur coal to utilities in the central Midwest and Ohio River Valley. It was a project, Schieffer liked to say, that made too much sense not to build.

"We go through fifty-seven communities on this project. The majority of them are supportive. There is one community on this line that is opposed to the project. And we've been pretty much told it's a bypass or no pass. And I can't get any further at the negotiation table with that kind of approach, because from our perspective a bypass is not something that works."

On a morning in the first week of February, Kevin Schieffer and the Rochester City Council held an open meeting to discuss a possible

agreement. My brother-in-law, Steve, and I arrived early enough to
help ourselves to sweet rolls and watch the room fill with council
members and farmers dressed for chores. Kathy arrived carrying a
grandchild still asleep in red pj's. The atmosphere was cordial;
everyone talked about the weather. But when the meeting began,
the seating arrangements resembled a map of Olmsted County: rural residents along the wall, Mayor Canfield and city council at the
table with a pair of Mayo representatives close at hand.

Earlier, the mayor had shook my hand, sticky from a caramel
bismarck. It was the first I'd seen him close up, and yet there was
something familiar in the jowly, eager face. It was a buyer's face,
beaming with acquisitiveness, the face of the city woman in Wood's
painting. The mayor looked ready to shop, eager to shower Schieffer with millions of taxpayers' dollars if only he'd build a bypass
around Rochester.

Schieffer, at one end of the table, flanked by city attorneys, began by explaining his conditions for building a bypass. First, the
city would have to pay most of the $75 to $200 million cost. Second, it would have to file its own federal application. And third,
landowners along the route would have to be brought into the ne-
gotiations. In short, if the city did the dirty work to build its own
bypass, Schieffer would run his trains on it.

"Kevin," said a city attorney, "when you started out, you said that
the emphasis of your agreement was to make the existing railroad
a better line. . . . In fact, your letter to Mayor Canfield says, 'If the
only value Rochester sees in this agreement is an immediate bypass, then we are all probably wasting our time.' We haven't gotten
past that point yet, have we?"

Schieffer hunched over the microphone. "Maybe the word 'immediate' is the, uh, operative word." But as he continued, Schieffer
spoke more rapidly and with less patience.

"We want to run our railroad. We have a right, I think, to run our
property like responsible businesses and do it with a very responsible approach to our neighbors. That's what this agreement is

about. I don't think we have to go out and tell someone else, 'We want to take your land instead of developing our own property because somebody thinks there might be a problem in the city.' If there's a problem in the city, then there's an opportunity for you to build. But before we establish that there is a problem, it's pretty hard for me to walk up to somebody's door and say, 'Hi. I'm from the railroad and we're going to take your land.' I've got to do that out West, and it's not fun."

The attorney frowned into his yellow pad. Then a councilman asked why Schieffer insisted that any agreement the railroad entered into with the city be cosigned by the Mayo Clinic.

"One thing that's become very apparent to me," Schieffer replied, "is that if Mayo wants an agreement, we'll have an agreement."

Some of us along the wall laughed. And a curious thing happened. The laughter spread from the spectators to the table itself, from the city council members to the otherwise dour-faced Mayo reps, until we were all guffawing, everybody enjoying a good laugh at the boss's expense. The only one not laughing was Kevin Schieffer, who seemed uncertain if he'd misspoken, not recognizing how awfully funny the obvious can be.

A few months before the Surface Transportation Board arrived in Rochester to hold public hearings on the DM&E proposal, a new "citizen-led coalition" emerged with the task of "generating a grassroots swell of protest" against the railroad. The founding board of Citizens to Stop the Coal Trains was largely composed of Mayo administrators and business leaders, some of whom had previously served on the steering committee. But in this new role, they did not "reference the bypass in public communication," insisting instead that they opposed the entire project. As an issue, the bypass had not generated much enthusiasm from exactly those city residents it was meant to save, possibly because "increased noise" and "vibrations" are lower on the emotional scale than losing one's family farm, and possibly because city residents felt ashamed to push their problem onto others. Eliminating the bypass from public discussion obviated that guilt and also made it possible for the group to receive $25,000 in in-kind support from the county board, which had adopted a "no-build" position. But the group's cover letter to the STB only opposed the upgrade through Rochester. Later, the group's cochair explained that he was not necessarily against the DM&E project, just the city route. "We have to have access to energy. I realize that," he said.

In November, the STB held its hearings at the Mayo Civic Center. Kathy King's group, now called Citizens Against Rochester's Bypass, carried flags printed with the coiled snake and motto of an earlier republic, "Don't Tread on Me." Their counterparts wore stop-sign buttons and Styrofoam hats that looked as if they'd been borrowed from the Bush campaign. One could not help being touched by the city group's innocence as they stepped one by one to the microphone to say that they did not want coal trains but neither did they want to force a bypass on their rural neighbors. It was this group, rather than the farmers, who made the nostalgic appeal to a mythic past.

"This has really been a sad afternoon and evening for me," said a former chief justice of the Minnesota Supreme Court, his voice quavering, "listening to the divisions between our community, one of the most remarkable communities in the world. To hear the hostility to Mayo, to see the divisions within our people, the farmers and the city people, it's just sad."

Time passes no slower in the country than in a city. It only seems that way because in the great cycle of seasons, of planting and harvesting, there is the illusion that days repeat themselves unerringly in a world without end. But they don't. Each is separate and irredeemable, and nothing is exactly the same.

A year later, after the City of Rochester allocated millions for a bypass and went fishing in Congress for the rest, the Surface Transportation Board ruled that the proposed bypass was not a feasible alternative. Predictably, the city appealed, but this too failed. It failed not because a bypass would have consumed a large swath of the countryside and the farms within but because of geology. The proposed route traversed large sections of karst topography with limestone fractures and hidden sinkholes that could have swallowed a locomotive. So in the end we won. But there was no victory celebration because nobody could believe that the project, or something like it, wouldn't pop up again in the future. I remember during the worst of times when a city councilman expressed the hope that "our country cousins" would understand this most "difficult" decision, and that we might return to that happy, golden yesteryear when everyone got along. It's nice to think so. Maybe the scars between city and country will heal over time; then again maybe not. A year before the STB's decision, my mother-in-law, Frances O'Neill, was diagnosed with cancer. She suffered, died, and was laid to rest in the cemetery beside St. Bridget's Church. And the last thing she knew, would ever know, was that those bastards were plotting a railroad out her bedroom window.

Wading the Big Two-Hearted

A river, the thinking goes, is as good as its name. And nowhere do the rivers run more evocative than in the Upper Peninsula of Michigan. There is the Yellow Dog, Salmon Trout, Ontonagon (four branches), and Manistique. But the most painfully beautiful of all streams, in name at least, is the Big Two-Hearted River. The words sound mysterious and vaguely Indian. They also form the title of Ernest Hemingway's classic story of trout fishing and angst in the north woods. Hemingway, who gleaned titles for his works from Ecclesiastes and John Donne, found this one ready-made on a map of Michigan. The river read like a line of his own clear prose.

Since 1925, when "Big Two-Hearted River" first appeared in *In Our Time,* Hemingway's river has been fixed in the literary landscape. A cold, fast-running trout stream, it rises in a cedar swamp to flow through burned-over country and the ruins of Seney, Michigan. My own first glimpse of it came when I was twenty and read in a dusty volume of *The Hemingway Reader* the story that

begins with Nick getting off the train at Seney. The town he expected to find has been devastated by fire. Nothing remains but
scorched earth and the heat-split foundation of the Mansion
House Hotel. Walking down the tracks, he finds the river still alive
and flowing beneath a bridge. *It stretched away, pebbly-bottomed
with shallows and big boulders and a deep pool as it curved away
around the foot of a bluff.*

Each year I reread the story and always it was the same—the Big
Two-Hearted more real than any actual stream. And I truly be-
lieved that Hemingway's river was there waiting to be found, if ever
I went looking.

The train doesn't stop at Seney anymore. And the town has crept
up to Highway M-24 to catch the summer tourist traffic. Twenty
years ago when Warner Brothers scouted locations for its lackluster
film version of the Nick Adams stories, they bypassed Seney altogether, settling for a more preserved town in northern Wisconsin.
Whatever rough charm Seney possessed in its heyday as a logging
town has long since given way to the brand of roadside functional-
ism best exemplified by the local mall—a rambling structure housing an IGA Market, the Golden Grill Cafe, and the U.S. Post Office,
all under one roof.

At the IGA, a Mennonite girl, her long hair drawn under an or-
gandy cap, toted up my camping supplies with one hand and
shoved them into a sack with the other. Then it was a short stroll
behind town to the railroad tracks. The rows of false-front saloons
and two of the biggest whorehouses in the lake states had disappeared when the last of the white pine was hauled away. Now
there were only a sawmill and some cottages along the railway.
Then nothing but the track bed of the Soo Line, heat-wavering as
it stretched off into the flat green country of northern Michigan.

I walked west along the tracks from Seney looking for the Big
Two-Hearted. A map wasn't necessary, the river's course having
been fixed in my mind for more than a decade. My affinity for the

story isn't unique. In the late sixties I once encountered another secret enthusiast on a coastal stream in California. He was an Aquar-
ian-age angler replete with waders and love beads who had
stopped to fish this tidal creek before heading up to the Bay Area
to score some business. We got to talking and when I mentioned
my Michigan origins, he started in on "Big Two-Hearted River." Together and in great detail we reconstructed Nick's river from memory—the big smooth rocks, the trout holding themselves in the current below the bridge, the kingfisher flying upstream. The fictional
angling took on more urgency and clarity than our own. The story
works that way.

Now I was excited to be walking the tracks toward the bridge
and at the same time afraid that the actual river would disappoint.

The river was there all right. Flowing along grassy banks, it
slipped beneath the iron bridge, a clear brown river louvered in
slats of light from the cracks between the cross ties.

I stood at midspan looking down into the water. The smell of
creosote rose from the bridge. In the story, Nick stands here a long
time watching trout swimming beside the log pilings. Then, picking up his heavy pack and rod case, he sets off across the hilly,
burned-out country to hit the river as far upstream as he can hike
in a day.

But I couldn't see any trout holding themselves in the river. The
river bottom was not pebbly, but sandy, and there were no boulders
to break up the current. Ahead, the river flowed through country
without a hint of a hill.

No kingfisher flew upstream.

Here was a river, certainly, but not the Big Two-Hearted.
Nowhere in the story is Nick's river alluded to by name. One just
assumes, wants to believe, it is identical to the title. It isn't.

Only one river flows near Seney, and it is the Fox. This was the
Fox River. The Big Two-Hearted, a real enough trout stream, lies
forty miles to the northeast in another county. To hike there from

Seney in a day, through swamp and thick woods, is flatly impossible. Which river, then, did Hemingway have in mind?

According to Hemingway's preeminent biographer, Dr. Carlos
Baker, the Fox is the story's germinal watershed. Hemingway had
been there in 1919, the summer of his twentieth year. He still
limped from a mortar wound received the year before on the Ital-
ian front, and recuperation took the form of trout fishing on
streams near his parents' cottage at Walloon Lake. A photograph
from that era shows the young Hemingway, wearing a cap and
shoulder-holster, smiling up from a cleaning table of unimpressive
trout. The final trip of the summer was to a river in the Upper
Peninsula. Ernest and two friends took the ferry across the straits
to St. Ignace and then the long, swaying train ride across the pine
flats to Seney. For a week they camped on the banks of the Fox
River above the town, catching trout and reveling in the absolute
freedom that would soon dissolve before the onslaught of employment and marriage.

Picking up a stone from the track bed, I skipped it across the
smooth surface of the Fox River. This may have been the river
Hemingway had in mind when he wrote the story, but it was not
the one I had imagined in all those years of vicarious wading.
Downhearted, I retraced my steps toward Seney.

"I've read the Hemingway story, and it's well written," said Jack
Riorden, "but, there isn't much fact about it. Remember at the be-
ginning when the baggageman throws Nick's pack from the train?
Well, that wasn't the baggageman at all. That was me."

We were sitting in a booth at the Golden Grill Cafe, talking
about the story over coffee. A trim man in steel-rimmed bifocals
and the tight smile of an Irish cleric, Riorden looks to be approaching the age of mandatory retirement. He is, in fact, eighty-
seven years old and had first come to Seney in 1916 to work for
the Duluth, South Shore & Atlantic Railroad as a telegraph op-

erator and assistant agent. In a place where people come and go, Riorden has stayed, and he speaks with a certain authority of years.

"When a train came in, my job was to pull a four-wheel cart up so the baggageman could hand down the baggage and express.

"And another thing, he's got it all wrong about the fire. There was a forest fire in 1917 or '18 and it burned the roof of the water tank. But it didn't burn the town. The town had burned down years before that."

Seney had indeed been destroyed by fire as Hemingway describes, but the fire occurred a generation earlier, in 1891. The town was rebuilt and then partially burned again in 1895 when the stumps and logging slash ignited in summer wildfires.

"When I came here," said Riorden, "maybe a hundred people were still living in Seney. Logging was still going on, but it wasn't for white pine. The white pine had run out by 1905. It was for what lumberjacks call short-stuff—pulpwood, fence posts, ties, and telephone poles. The Grodin Hotel was still standing. What Hemingway calls the Mansion House Hotel was the White House. Only it didn't burn. It was moved down the road to Germfask."

Riorden finished his coffee and looked around for a girl to fill his cup again.

"It's a good story," he conceded, "but the facts aren't straight."

Literature, of course, is not a matter of mere facts. I liked to think myself a better critic than Jack Riorden because I understood that the distortion of geography in "Big Two-Hearted River" was purposeful and added to the story. Still, there was the matter of expectations. I needed to believe that Nick's river had a counterpart in actuality—a river that was pebbly and fast-running over big smooth rocks.

Some distance from Seney, a state forest sign stands beside the bridge on Highway L-407. Yellow lettering is routed onto the wooden sign:

BIG TWO-HEARTED RIVER
IMMORTALIZED BY ERNEST HEMINGWAY

Nobody, however, calls the river by its full name. Locals speak of it simply as the Two-Heart, reserving the "Big" to distinguish this river from the "Little" Two-Hearted further to the east. The shortened form is not nearly so poetic, and Hemingway, who probably never saw the river, knew a good title when he heard one.

The watershed of the Two-Heart lies in northern Luce County, a primitive area of lakes and pine forests with sparsely populated settlements like Deer Park and Pine Stump Junction. Rising in clear, spring-fed lakes, the river's three major tributaries angle in from opposing compass points to become the Two-Hearted. The river takes on the color of the cedar swamps and tamarack forests in its path, so that by the time the Two-Hearted passes beneath the bridge, the river has darkened and covers the pebbly bottom like a fine shellac.

My shadow makes a slight bump on the bar of shade the bridge span throws across the river. Hemingway may have never set eyes on the Two-Heart, but he certainly imagined it. Curving around a steep bank of birch and cedar, the river piles up against big rocks to make white rents in the slick stretch of water. All the details of Nick's river come together. At any moment, a kingfisher will make its obligatory flight upstream.

Fly rod in hand, I strike off for the upper Two-Heart down a sandy road that stretches off through the jack pine, the trees nicely spaced with ferns growing up between the pines. It's a hot afternoon. The heat fairly radiates off the white surface of the road. Already I'm sweating beneath a Duluth pack overloaded with a camping outfit from an era when the mark of an outdoorsman was the sheer volume of junk he could haul into the woods.

Turning south toward the river, the road climbs up and around forested ridges. I rest my pack on a cut bank and watch a swallow-tail butterfly flutter down the hot road. A wind rips through the treetops, and the road moves in and out of shadow. The river cannot be far off.

This is the Michigan woods that Hemingway was trying to write about in 1924. That was in Paris, and living in another country seemed to sharpen the image of his own. Mornings he would often write at a café where he wasn't known, and then walk to the Musée du Luxembourg in the afternoons to look at the French Impressionists' paintings. In a letter to Gertrude Stein, an early mentor, he mentioned a long story he had written about trout fishing and how in it he was "trying to do the country like Cézanne."

The story is a somber reflection of the trip Ernest had taken five years earlier to the Fox River. Not only is the river altered, but Nick is now alone as he hikes upriver from Seney and makes his camp beside a meadow where the river runs into a swamp. He cooks his supper and reminisces about an earlier trip where the camp had been filled with other voices. Now in the darkening woods the sound of his own voice alarms him. The next day, Nick wakes early to catch grasshoppers for bait before the dew dries off their wings. Wading downstream, he hooks a big trout and loses it. He catches two more before the river narrows into a dense swamp. Nick turns back, feeling some aversion to deep wading among the tangled cedars where trout could be hooked but not landed and the fishing would be a *tragic adventure.*

That is all that happens in "Big Two-Hearted River." But the way Hemingway wrote about country was something new. The short, simple words blend together like flat brushstrokes of pigment on a landscape full of light and shadow. The graceful repetition of words creates a strange sense of depth: *There was the meadow, the river and the swamp. There were birch trees in the green of the swamp on the far side of the river.*

The road dips down, and I cross the North Branch of the Two-Heart on a plank bridge and climb to a grassy clearing at the confluence of the North Branch and main river. Grasshoppers fly off through the dry grass like popping corn. But they are too small this early in the summer and not worth flailing after. Here then is the meadow and the river, but other Nicks have been here and left old campfires heaped with charred tin cans.

Further up the road is a better campsite, a sandy bluff where the river cuts close in a horseshoe curve. I stake out my old canvas tent on a bed of pine needles and push a freshly cut pole up the center so the sides straighten out and the door flaps overlook the river. The oxbow affords a 160° view of the Two-Heart, lost elsewhere in solid alder. Downstream, a tree has fallen across the river, and I can hear its branches cutting into the surface of the water.

Evening comes on slowly this far north. As I feed the campfire, the last of the daylight climbs up the trunks of birch trees across the river. I open a can of spaghetti and another of beans and wonder how many young men in khaki shirts and impossible packs make this pilgrimage, their lips silently reciting each scene as it is reenacted. Nick Hiking Across the Pine Plain. Nick Finding the Grasshoppers. Nick Opening the Cans of Spaghetti and Beans.

"Big Two-Hearted River" lends itself to this kind of ritualization because its hero is himself so terribly methodical. Nick is bent upon reliving an earlier trip when he was not so unnerved. From the moment he gets off the train, Nick wants so much to feel *all the old feeling*. The grasshoppers must be a certain size and color. The coffee must be brought to boil a certain way. Nick seems bent on reliving some early fishing trip that he had made. Or that he had dreamed.

In "Now I Lay Me," a story Hemingway wrote after "Big Two-Hearted River" but set earlier in the Nick Adams chronology, Nick has been wounded in a night shelling and is convinced that if he allows himself to fall asleep his soul will slip effortlessly from his body. He devises various methods to stay awake. He prays. He thinks of all the girls he has known. But mostly he recalls trout streams he has fished and meticulously wades them in his mind, starting near their source and working downstream. When he had gone through all the streams he can remember, he devises imaginary streams.

The river Nick fishes in "Big Two-Hearted River" may be one of the imagined streams that help Nick make it through the night or an actual river he has returned to. In any case, the waters are tonic to Nick's shaken spirit. The river is not, however, some simple recuperative spring, a trout-stocked Lourdes. There are deep nightmare pools where the old fear wells up. And the darkest, deepest pool of all is the swamp.

In the morning, I am up early. The sun is still low, the woods in long shadows, and there is this river running below the bluff. Flopping in my waders down the riverine forest, I break out into a slot of open sky above the Two-Heart. The river here takes a slight step over a sandstone ledge into a foamy pool. Accelerating as it slides over the smooth rock ledge, the river takes the plunge in bright, oxygenated sheets that spill across the pool below. A likely spot for the Big Two-Hearted Trout.

Picking my way around rocks, I wade the shallow stretch below the pool, the river frigid, even through the waders. False casting enough line to reach upriver, I address the fly to the deep water below the ledge and come up tight on a trout. It is a midget brook trout that comes easily, surfacing across the water to the net, nothing like the broad, salmon-like monsters that bend Nick's fly rod double. In the spring, anadromous rainbow trout, or steelhead, ascend the Two-Heart from Lake Superior to spawn. But aside from a few lingering rainbows, this is brook trout water. Dampening my hand, as Nick would do, I release the brookie and follow the current downstream like so much flotsam.

After he left Paris and returned to this country as its resident literary lion, Hemingway lost interest in Michigan. The years were
spent divided between the Florida Keys, Cuba, and finally Idaho.
The north woods, he said, had changed too much. The wilderness
he had known as a boy was gone, minced into lakefront lots and
timber cuttings.

Maybe so, but the Two-Hearted remains the river we want it to
be. Most of its watershed lies within the boundaries of Lake Superior State Forest, and the remaining private lands are held in large
parcels by logging concerns and a handful of venerable sporting
clubs. Since 1973, the Two-Hearted has been designated a Wilderness River by the state with subsequent restrictions on logging,
road building, and cabin construction along its banks. With few access points and countless logjams, the Two-Hearted is a river that
resists the hordes of canoeists and shore fishermen. You have to slip
in and wade it.

At the confluence with the North Branch, I turn left and slosh
up the lesser stream. No singular swamp intersects the Two-
Hearted such as Nick confronts, but stretches like the North
Branch possess the same dark, constricting qualities. There are always plenty of trout in streams like this, scarcely fished trout leading unlikely lives in brief pockets of water. The going is torturous,
cedars crisscrossing the river, the banks unwieldy with timber.

I aim a short cast above a cedar snag, and the current sweeps
the fly into a pocket of still water behind the log. The line tightens. I swing the rod back and set the hook. The trout makes a
short, heartening run before it sags in my net. A nice-sized
brookie, its sides brilliantly flecked with vermilion dots and
golden coronas.

Pleased with myself, I slip the trout into the creel and work my
way further up the North Branch, hauling myself over logjams and
raising clouds of mosquitoes. When an open stretch of water finally
presents itself, I quickly break my leader on a submerged root. I'm
annoyed, but what I really want is to feel some deep reaction

against this wading, some link with the story so that my heart tightens with *all the old feeling.*

The feeling never comes. The river is the same, but not the fisherman. Maybe that is why Hemingway never came back to Michigan when he was no longer a young man afraid of the darkening woods. People change in ways the country doesn't.

With the one good brookie for lunch, I walk back to the confluence. I will go back to camp now, fry up the trout and read again the story that begins with Nick getting off the train at Seney.

I head up the river trail, and a ratcheting song overflows the banks as a kingfisher swoops upstream.

Snow on the Mountains

The train pulled away and followed the river up the terraced valley and into a narrow gorge in the outer mountains of the Alaska Range. When the last car passed out of sight, I looked down from the depot as the Nenana broadened out from the canyon into many braided channels on the wide gravel flats below. The wind was picking up, moving cloud shadows down the high white bluffs and across the gravel bars. As the river came out from under a shadow into hard daylight, I could just make out the silty turbulence in each channel, the gray pulsing of arteries flowing north into the Tanana, the Yukon, emptying into an Asian sea.

The baggageman had set my pack at the end of the platform. Shouldering it, I walked past the depot and the Healy Hotel and down the spur road to the highway. Healy was a coal mining town. All of the buildings were painted the same depressing brown and gray as the depot except for the state trooper's trailer, which had set itself off from the overwhelming bleakness with a white picket fence. A dog began to bark, the only sound but the wind.

On the highway outside of town, a young couple in a van stopped and placed me among their baggage. Then we headed north, cresting frost heaves with a frantic momentum.

"In a decade all this," the driver gestured with his hand toward the unstable horizon, "will be developed. Car washes and trailer parks."

"That's why we left Boulder," his wife added. "That's why we've come here."

She was pregnant, her face luminous next to her husband's hairiness. They had arrived in Alaska to find the Matanuska Valley filled up. Now they were heading for Circle, he explained, before all the land was gone.

From the louvered window I could see only that nothing had changed. Mountains and river and the small breaks in the trees where someone had made a start then gave up.

We stopped at the turn-off for the Stampede Trail, a poor excuse for a road running seventy miles west to abandoned mines in the Kantishna Hills. The driver helped pull my pack from the van. Then he stood in the wind fingering his beard, thinking of a pronouncement, but he only says: Good luck with the fishing. Then they were off, driving down the highway toward Circle, furiously.

The Stampede Trail parallels the Outer Range. As the road climbed out of an aspen gulch onto the high tundra plain, more of the mountains showed and the sky seemed closer to the ground. The walking was good. The weather had been dry the last few weeks and the surface of the road had baked to a hard, white dust. The mud holes in the low spots were circumscribed with sticks and mill ends where a tire had once sunk to its axle.

No more than six miles to the south, the mountains kept me company. They rise vertically from the broad plain to five and six thousand feet, dark green veins of spruce on the lower slopes showing the route of snow melt. But there was no snow yet on the gray talus peaks, even in the sheltered pockets. Beyond these outer mountains, however, rises the Alaska Range proper which stands like a Great Wall against storms blown north from the Gulf of Alaska, and on whose peaks it is perpetual winter.

Not far from here, at Dry Creek, anthropologists digging on a bluff over the creekbed found the coals of ancient campfires, and mingled in the ashes were the bones of Pleistocene horse and long-horned bison. The last glacial epoch did not extend north of this range, so that while the rest of the continent lay ice-bound, these plains were green. Hunters newly arrived from Asia trekked the foot of these slopes, eating their kill in the firelight of nights twelve thousand years ago. Twelve thousand years of these mountains, this sky.

In 1972 my first wife and I were new to the country and to each other. Equipped with a vision of life acquired mostly from books which promised that if we only lived simply our lives would be simple and carefree, we staked five acres of land on Panguingue Creek and began felling logs to build a home. But we did not finish that summer or the next. When it was finally done and the door hung, we forgot why we had ever started. That was four years ago. Strange now to be back on this road, alone, wondering what remained of the cabin or if it, like the marriage, had collapsed from the accumulated weight of intervening winters.

The road dipped slightly and I headed off, following a trail along a ridge where the narrow valley falls away. From the crest I caught the first glimpse of the creek, a thin ribbon glinting sunlight through a canopy of yellow scrub willow. The trail descended in a hand-over-hand, tree-grabbing slide to the bottom. Bushwhacking through alders, I followed the sound of water. Then I saw it again, a rock-stuffed creek descending the valley in several pitches, linked by smooth stretches that showed clear to the pebbled bottom as if there was no water. I crossed on a rock shelf where grayling held themselves in the current, the larger fish centering themselves among the fry. A rock tilted under my weight and the grayling scattered like quicksilver.

On this side of the creek the willows were overgrown, the trail lost. I felt an aversion to willow thickets where the dim light breaks a sickly yellow through the leaves and exposed roots catch your feet. In such close quarters with branches closing overhead and behind, there is no room to maneuver.

From the pack, I took out the revolver I had wrapped in a wool shirt to keep it from chafing my back. It was a borrowed gun, a heavy Italian-made .44 magnum, meant to outweigh my own fears. Cocking the hammer, I loaded all but the firing chamber then threaded the holster onto my belt. Yet when I came upon the moist heap of crushed leaves and blueberries on the sandy ground, the old fear itself, the revolver seemed weightless and insubstantial. With no one to tell me all the tired bear stories, the maulings and mutilations, the fables and out-right lies, I tell them to myself.

The spoor, however, was cold, the animal a day or two distant in the hills. In a quaking voice, I began to sing, pitifully out of key, as birds sing to define territory, to define a swath out of the willow break and into the comparatively open spruce forest of the south slope.

The cabin was set back on a rise above the creek. Coming upon it suddenly, I was startled by the axe propped against the door, the neat pile of firewood under the eave so that I almost called out. But the axe was mine. There was no one here. The door was latched shut just as I had left it four years ago.

I pushed open the door and the floor gleamed bits of broken glass. A chair lay on its side amid the debris. Most likely a bear had broken the front window, sampled the furniture and left. Otherwise, nothing had changed. A magazine my wife had brought along to read four summers ago lay spread open on the table alongside a list of provisions never purchased. I slipped out of the pack and placed the holster on the table. I felt strangely intrusive here, like one of the archeologists digging at Dry Creek, sifting through the effects of people I don't know. The cabin offered few artifacts from which to construct the lives of its builders. The overriding question was: Why did they leave?

Near the end of that first summer, we had cut, peeled and hauled to the site all the logs for the cabin walls. My wife often paused in her labors to document on film what she felt would otherwise pass quickly into reminiscence. A photograph she took at the time showed me astride a logjam of cabin logs, a doltish grin on my face, happier than I had ever been in my life. We should have finished then, but we didn't. Climbing out of the valley in the fall, we'd left the walls holding up nothing but sky.

Chores suggested themselves. After sweeping up the broken glass, I repaired the gaping window with a makeshift sheet of plastic. We had built up from the creek to keep watch on the Outer Range and the weather. In the mountains, fronts are in constant mutation, forming and darkening and passing over as if in a time-lapse sequence. Even now dun-colored clouds were spilling through the gaps in the range though the view through the plastic was diffused, shades of earth and sky bleeding together.

With rain threatening and supper to catch, there wasn't a moment to lose. In the pre-storm half-light, grayling were rising all down the sleek stretches of stream, dimpling the surface of the water. I sat on the bank and rigged a willow switch with monofilament and a tiny hook dressed up to imitate a black gnat. Short on tactics, I started downstream, walking one bank then the other, dropping my fly into calm eddies behind boulders, sometimes spooking a fish that torpedoed upstream through shallow water to new cover. Without weight or tapered line, casting presented a real problem. Standing on a slippery rock, I lay the fly in midstream and let the current carry it under a willow overhang. A fish took it, jumped once, and was suddenly alive in my hand. I splashed ashore, examining the grayling's mica-flecked sides and high dorsal fin. A tap on its skull with my knife and the fish went rigid.

The second summer, we'd returned to the cabin and picked up our tools as if the intervening winter never occurred. Winter had made a difference, of course, and before long we found ourselves inventing side-trips and excursions, sunny days to cache away for the dark of the next winter. Soon the cabin was heavily mortgaged with day hikes and berry picking in the berm piles along the Stampede Trail. After a day hauling lumber for the roof, my wife just sat down among the wood shavings and announced that she was tired of it, tired of the work and mosquitoes, tired of the taste of Velveeta and hardtack (which she called "heart attack"), but mostly tired of looking up at these valley walls knowing that beyond them the briefest of summers was slipping away. She proposed a trip to the ocean where the silver salmon were running. So we went and, sure enough, when we returned, snow was falling.

A dry oxbow offered a shortcut from my rock-hopping route down the creek, so I followed it inland. In the spring, this channel would be underwater, and even now dank-smelling puddles remained in the low spots. The mud of one such puddle held calligraphy of claw points and toes radiating from a massive depression. Bears are solitary enough animals that the print could have been made by the same bear that broke into the cabin. The valley slopes were too narrow, the creek too much of a highway to doubt that we would put off meeting indefinitely. So I was glad when the willows opened up and the creek was there again, only deeper and undercutting the bank.

The current carried my fly into a deep pocket beneath a fallen spruce. The line suddenly went taut, the fish making downstream toward the submerged branches. Without a reel, I walked backwards from the creek and pulled the fish ashore. It wasn't a grayling this time but a Dolly Varden trout, a beautiful fish, actually a char, mottled sides of vermilion and white and an underside of pure gold. I sapped it then dipped it back in the water to wash off the sand. In the low light, the colors were still brilliant.

"But there's nothing to do here."

Without her presence, I found myself making my wife's arguments: the isolation, the suffocating quality of the woods. When the cabin was finished, nothing remained but to live there and that was the hardest task of all. Pregnant at the end of that third summer, she was often sick to her stomach, waiting out the rains and the overwhelming silence while I ran off to do anything but share the silence with her. We both knew by then that the vision had faded, the reason for staying, but I was stalling. I was stalling until she delivered a child. A child would surely moor us to this valley.

In Fairbanks, in midwinter, she'd gone into labor, three months premature. The early morning drive to the hospital remained fixed in my mind, an inversion of white landscape and dark sky. I talked as I drove, full of optimism she wouldn't share. At 7:30 A.M. our son was born, and nameless, died an hour later. Not much time by any measure. A day later, driving back from the hospital, we said very little but understood implicitly that we would leave Alaska.

All down the creek, fish appeared to be rising, yet it was only the rain. As light diminished, the rain fell harder, filling the woods with a din. Already I had the sick feeling of having wandered too far. Winding the line around the willow switch, I picked up my fish and started upstream. Yellow leaves soaked me to the skin. A bear was anywhere in the thicket. Lightning flashed, a delayed rumbling, and I started running.

The valley had become a single element through which I was swimming toward the cabin, which suddenly loomed ahead like an island. Inside, I changed clothes and fired up the airtight. The sheet-metal stove buckled loudly in the rising heat. Soon coffee was boiling and the fish fried up nicely in a big iron skillet. My hunger was unreasonable.

The light was going out in the west. The Outer Range had disappeared, the valley submerged below a cloud cover that seemed the rippled surface of another world. I lit a kerosene lamp and listened to the steady drumming of rain on the roof. There *was* nothing to do here. I said it over and over to myself, a kind of mantra, and the more I said it the easier it was to accept. The cabin walls could never keep out the forest because they were the forest. I had never stood still long enough here to let the woods, the valley roll over me like a wave as they did now, and it was a kind of relief.

Snuffing out the wick, I curled in my sleeping bag close to the stove, alternately roasting and shivering. It was a fitful night, full of starts and awakenings in the dark, the screeching of real owls and imagined bears stalking close by in the woods.

Waking once in the dark, I thought I could see the mountains through the window, but the night was moonless, too dark to see anything. One mountain, though, I saw clearly in my mind. It was the beginning of a ridge rising out of the Savage River which I had climbed my last summer in Alaska. It had been a difficult climb, but the view improved with elevation: green glacial valleys, shimmering veins of river, and the backbone of the Alaska Range. The mountain leveled off at the top into a green ridge, windblown and covered with primrose, a divide from which the earth seemed to fall away. I climbed to a cairn breaking out of the moss campion and could see among the brown hills to the north the narrow valley cut by Panguingue Creek. Holding onto the rock with one hand, I took the ashes of my first-born out of a small box and held them in the other until the wind carried them like snow onto the bare slopes. There had been no service that day but the wind, the primrose, and the river below in the canyon.

Morning broke cool, the cabin floor sharply lit. The rain had stopped, and in its place awakened flies busied themselves against the plastic-covered window. Stiffly, I dressed and lit a fire in the stove. Blueberry pancakes were the order for breakfast.

Forgetting the gun, I walked slowly towards the creek, gathering berries in a tin plate. The day was heartbreakingly beautiful: blue-washed sky, raindrops glistening on willows, the creek running fast and full. The Outer Range was plainly visible, talus slopes dusted with the first fine snow of the coming winter. The air was crisp enough for it to remain and soon be buried beneath the strata of subsequent snows until the lengthening days of another summer peel away the layers until this first covering melts and runs off the slopes and into a watershed that feeds the Nenana and the Tanana and the Yukon and flows at last into an ocean that covers the world.

Touching Bottom

The woman I've been seeing lately won't eat wild meat. Her ex-husband had been a hunter, and perhaps he'd been brutal in other ways or simply a bad cook, but his memory has tainted all wild game for her. This seemed a shame the first time I invited her for a duck dinner and she pushed aside the main course to concentrate on the acorn squash, brussels sprouts, and wild rice. She's a big-boned woman with a rope of wheat-colored hair down her back and vulnerable blue eyes. She's thinking, she says, of becoming a vegetarian.

I have noticed how often friends emerge from divorce only to immerse themselves in some new obsession. They drink too much or run marathons or give themselves over to a breathless fundamentalism. My friend and I pursue separate diets but share the same hunger. Obviously, she hasn't learned from her mistakes because I'm allowed to stay over on the nights before I go duck hunting.

4:30 in the morning. After batting the alarm clock off the nightstand, there is the heavy weight of inertia to deal with. Lately, I cannot so much as get out of bed without screening a private newsreel of the past that always ends with why I am sleeping in a strange bed. Also, there is this cat lodged between my legs.

Pulling myself from the warm covers, I dress quietly in the dark. The woman sighs, rolls over on her belly and pretends to sleep. Outside the bedroom window, the streetlight illuminates a trapezoid of bare elms and sidewalk. The cat cries by the door. Boots in hand, I pick up my canvas coat and gun case in the hallway and slip out the door before the cat can make its getaway.

The highway flows through the October darkness, steeply banked with stubble fields and woodlots. Farmyards sail past in the circle of their arc lights. Fiddling with the radio, I dial through storms of static and settle finally upon a distant country station. "Heartaches Till Dawn" is the name of the show, and a plaintive hillbilly voice solicits my phone-in requests.

At the Fox Coulee landing, duck hunters are already gathering in the predawn gloom. Most of the pickup trucks have Minnesota plates, the hunters having crossed the state line to hunt the river bottoms with its byzantine sloughs and tangled beaver canals. Waiting their turn at the boat launch, they hunch in heated cabs or stand outside playing flashlights over the swirling current. Every so often, someone asks what time it's getting to be.

Spotting Richard's blue station wagon, I slide in beside his retriever, a black Labrador with grinning white teeth and minstrel-show eyes. Richard passes me a cup of coffee from his Thermos and a gooey breakfast roll and then proceeds to outline the situation. Heavy fall rains have raised the river too high to wade, so we'll need to beg a lift across the channel. Richard steps outside and hails a party of Minnesotans cozying into their camouflaged jonboat with its mesh blind and big Evinrude. Through the windshield, I watch him gesturing as he re-outlines the situation. The men in the boat have thick, blank faces and apparently no necks. They look at Richard and then follow his outstretched arm to the car where the dog and I are waiting. In a single motion, they shake their heads and roar down the river.

The woods on the far shore have begun to take shape in the silvery half-light when we finally convince a coon trapper to ferry us across the channel. He's been waiting for sunrise to legally make his sets along the riverbank and now decides there's sufficient daylight. We clamber aboard, the black Lab riding masthead on the bow, my boots resting against a tangle of traps and chains on the bottom of the boat. As the trapper ferries us across the misting, slightly stygian river, no one mentions how we are going to get back.

Ashore, we set off through the woods single file, the terrain presenting itself as a series of blowdowns and water hazards. Beavers have cut the willows into sharp pungi sticks and moated the bottomlands with interconnecting canals and ponds so that every inch of land is an island within an island. Wading a beaver canal, the black water rising sharply to my waders, I nearly tumble over a sunken log. I wrench my foot loose and bubbles of methane gas break the surface with the pungency of rotten eggs.

Approaching the pond we plan to hunt, I can make out another party of hunters in silhouette, their anchored decoys riding high in the water. It's nearly dawn, so Richard and I split up on either side of an inlet, flickering our flashlights to keep from blasting each other in a crossfire. There's nothing much to do but wait. The sky turns a delft blue, and I busy myself leading blackbirds on the horizon. A breeze comes up and shifts the decoys around so they no longer appear to be on speaking terms.

From the distance comes the far-off thunder of shooting. High above the treetops, an immense flight of geese is moving southward, the din of collective honking carried before it. The angle of birds is perfectly formed, the point throwing a wake of two equal lines across the sky. Crouching down in the buttonbrush, I wait to see if the geese will come within range. They are still impossibly high when the hunters across the pond open up. They must be firing automatics with the plugs removed. It sounds like a small war.

In the midst of this barrage, Richard stands up from his cover and yells over the water.

"What's that?" one of the gunners asks as the shooting tapers off.

"I said," Richard bellows into the sudden quiet, "that you're a pack of assholes!"

We stalk off through the woods and decide to split up. I make a long, careful stalk up a beaver canal that opens into a wide marsh but come up empty-handed. The morning is heating up and my woolens begin to chafe. I sit on the wreckage of an old beaver lodge and eat a mashed sandwich and don't see the pair of mallards dropping in until their wings whistle overhead. I swing on the drake, and the bird crumples into the marsh. Wading out, I pick up the drake and slip it warm and heavy beneath my arm like a loaf of bread. When I look back, the pond has already healed over, a few downy feathers floating on the still surface.

Much later, Richard shows up with a pair of greenheads hung from a sling around his neck. Uncertain the retrieving is over, the black Lab leaps up again and again to sniff the dead birds and snap her teeth. We reach the round pothole to find the hunting party already departed, their decoys left anchored in the water. Before we leave, Richard wades out and cuts all the cords.

At the riverbank, the channel looks lower to me, a translucent brown in the daylight, and I feel certain we can wade it. Richard is first. He cinches the belt tight around the top of his waders, slips into the river, shotgun held aloft, and begins working his way sideways to the current. Halfway across, Richard takes a long step and angles into the river, water pouring into his waders. His hat floats away as he kicks to shore.

Stripping off his wet clothes, Richard shouts encouragement from the other side as I slide down the grassy bank into the water. His dog, alone now, begins to whine and frantically pace the shore

I have so recently abandoned. Finally the Lab lunges in and swims past me to the opposite bank. On tip-toe, I feel tentatively for the drop-off, losing heart because I know it's there. Stepping forward, I sink, weighted down with shells, into what seems like the Atlantic Trench. The river seals overhead in a wash of dim light until the bottom rises to meet me, and I push off, breaching the surface, and reemerge on the far shore.

The next time I cross the channel, I'm swaddled in a life preserver worn beneath my canvas coat. But the river has fallen in the un-expected warmth of the late autumn and the crossing is easy. Richard's Lab paddles ahead of us as usual, springing up the bank and shaking the river from her glossy black coat. Excited by the rich, humus smell of the river bottoms, she begins to circle, mak-ing false starts for the woods until we're clear of the channel. She doesn't appear to be dying.

We follow the distant trail of her barking through wild grape and prickly ash until we reach the round pothole we'd hunted ear-lier in the season. Richard takes the shovel I have carried and starts to dig through black muck and rootage. The shovel makes a suck-ing sound each time it lifts free of the wet earth. Richard is by now sweating, his movements jagged, and when he reaches solid clay he heaves the shovel into the tall grass. He calls the dog over, gently slips her collar off and puts it in his coat pocket.

The dog is dying of a melanoma, a cancer that has bloomed and spread in her throat, slowly starving her to death. The veterinarian who examined the dog a week before suggested a lethal injection right there and then in his office. It seemed the thing to do. Most of us cannot bear putting an end to the things we care about and so willingly give up the task to strangers. But the dog had a quaking fear of the vet's office with its menagerie of fatal odors, so Richard declined, deciding to take the dog's life himself where she had seemed best defined, here in the river bottoms.

He breaks open a cellophaned dog snack and places it on the ground beside the hole he has dug. While the dog laps it up, he loads the .22 rifle and backs away to aim. But the dog has an unsettling way of looking up at him as she eats.

I am sitting on a tree stump, looking out over the pond and wishing for invisibility.

"Call her," Richard says.

My mouth is too dry to whistle, so I face the dog and call out her name. She glances up from her meal before I can turn away and fixes me with a look free of implication.

The rifle shot claps over the pond. A pair of wood ducks whirr up from the windfall where they've been hiding, and I follow their flight as they clear the pond and disappear behind the dark smudge of bordering woods.

This is a weekend that I have my daughter. Halloween is a few days away and she's undecided about what to be. She watches unsqueamishly while I pluck the feathers from a plump mallard I'm sending home with her as a little peace offering. Then, declaring her boredom, she picks up an iridescent blue primary feather and puts it in her hair. The rest of the day, she wears it around the apartment, imagining she's an Indian.

Later, we drive to my ex-wife's house, but she's not there. I'm early or she's late. Whatever, I sit down on the back porch stoop and watch my daughter swing on a tire swing hanging from a big walnut tree. All of this is just too familiar.

Her mother drives up with a carload of groceries. Of late, she's taken up racquetball and looks flushed and beautiful, a walking testimonial to self-assertion. I hand over the duck in a plastic bag, a husbandly gesture that seems, under the circumstances, absurd. But she is cordial, thanking me and sweeping up the gift with the grocery bags. For a moment, there is an awkward straining for talk so this won't seem like a hostage exchange. I try to think of something to say, but the words only come out faster and louder until

I'm shouting. On that cue, she whisks daughter and groceries inside, the back door slams, and they're gone.

By November, migrations are no longer pouring down the northern flyway. The ducks you missed a month ago are lolling in a warm bayou while you cheerlessly watch football and contemplate another midwestern winter. Still, there is always the question of one last trip to the river bottoms, knowing ahead of time it will be useless, and yet necessary to certify that it was.

A gray sky filled with shifting light hangs over the channel as I make the crossing. Pan ice has formed in scallops along the shore while the beaver ponds and canals have all frozen over. The ice shudders and cracks as I slowly cross a clear pane above black water. It's an edgy feeling, like walking on a skylight that might suddenly give way and drop you unannounced into a dimly lit room swirling with pike and old leaves.

Making the rounds of frozen potholes, I soon get the idea I'm alone in here. But there's a lead of open water running in one of the sloughs. The wind dies in the trees, and from around the bend I hear the quivering chatter of northern mallards. I bring the wooden duck call, strung from a lanyard around my neck, to my lips and give the Highball, a raucous call like the self-propelled laugh of a bore: Ha-Ha-Ha-Ha-Ha.

Like ourselves, ducks are gregarious and want to be let in on the joke, no matter how awful. This flock must be the exception or they've heard this one before because when I try to sneak up to them through the dry grass, they fly up like a window shade. As they head for the big water, I think: That's it.

Then from around a horsehoe bend a straggler calls, a hen mallard. Crouching in the grass, I answer with the Lonesome Hen Call, the torch song of waterfowlers. Each time I do, something like an echo answers from around the bend. Laments, real and contrived, pass from one end of the slough to the other until I feel a connection of some importance is at hand. I've almost lost interest in shooting the hen. But when she flies around the bend to see who's calling, that's exactly what I do.

The bird plummets, the sky no longer buoying her up, and drops like a stone into the open slough. I am already up and crashing through the reeds to reach the riverbank, but when I get there she's gone.

You always feel remorse crippling a bird, although the end is the same. Whether it ends up as a meal for you or a scavenging fox is a distinction the bird is unlikely to care about. Still, you want to redeem yourself.

I wade out into the icy slough, the bottom muck solid beneath me, hoping the duck will rise long enough for me to finish her off. Flurries are blowing across the water and my hands are going numb. I think how much easier this would be with a good bird dog to sniff out the hen as she heads for cover in the reeds. I begin to wish that Richard's dog was not dead but revived beside me. And then I wish that I had never made the shot in the first place. And a whole flood of wishes follows.

Preoccupied, I nearly fail to see the crippled hen surface. The dusky brown head bobs just beyond the reeds, and very slowly I raise the shotgun barrel. But the mallard sees this movement, sees me, and for an instant fixes me in her stare before diving under.

Then the slough is utterly empty in the blowing snow. I wade ashore and wait on into the darkening afternoon, knowing I'm not going to see the hen again, knowing I've already consigned her to that long, long list of things done badly that no amount of wishing will undo.

Beyond Whales

We came down the outer coast of Baranof Island at night in eight-foot seas. With no stabilizers, nothing to counter the swells rolling off the Gulf of Alaska, the ship pitched and wallowed through the darkness. Next morning, though, the horizon was restored, my cabin strangely calmed. I stepped onto the balustraded deck to find the ship anchored at the end of a long, fjordlike arm of Whale Bay, surrounded by lush green mountains rising into the clouds. Descending the companionway, I found the captain of the research vessel *Alpha Helix* in the mess room, weary from his watch but brightening over coffee as he spoke of whales blowing at the entrance to the bay.

All day we sheltered out of the storm until evening, when the sea calmed enough for us to cross the bay in a small rubber boat to explore its other arm. We passed hanging valleys filled with snow and the long, ropey strands of waterfalls—half a dozen in one cirque—gushing down from the clouds. The arm was eighty fathoms deep and steeply canted, its banks dense and jungly, a dream forest out of Rousseau. It ended, miles from the sea, in an estuary stream that poured out of a crack in the forest. We watched a brown bear grazing beside the stream, tearing up wild celery roots and chewing them like cud. One of our party, a wildlife photographer, wanted to move closer for a better shot. "You can never get close enough," she said, although we seemed plenty close to me. The tide was in, so we tilted back the outboard and rowed up the cobbled streambed until the bear arose and, pushing a massive shoulder through the greenery, disappeared.

Now we were heading back to the ship. At the mouth of the bay, I braced for oncoming rollers, but the storm had left behind only gentle swells and a pearly twilight. The *Alpha Helix* was visible in the distance. I took the walkie-talkie from its waterproof bag to radio our imminent return when the photographer pointed at two white puffs of vapor rising off the horizon like exclamation points. Changing course, we raced toward the geysers until we could see a pair of black hillocks beneath them curving purposefully through the water. Humpback whales, a cow and calf, judging from their size. Humpbacks are the "singing" whales with pleated mouths full of baleen and long, oarlike flippers.

There is an etiquette to whale watching, a threshold of distance beyond which lies harassment, and we were close to crossing it. But a whale spout is a terrific come-on, like a searchlight above a grand opening; the whale's great size is itself a form of magnanimity. Despite their having been hunted for millennia by men in small boats, probably in this very bay (100,000 whales were killed in Alaskan waters in the 1870s alone), we drew closer, as if to enlarge ourselves, trusting that among whales good intentions count for something.

The next time the whales blew, we heard the blast from the blowhole and felt the cool mist of their breath on our cheeks. A smell like rancid seaweed hung in the air. Then the whales sounded, diving vertically with a characteristic upstroke of the tail.

A beautiful and emblematic sight—immense horizontal flukes planing off the water and upending in a gesture as meaningful and final as a hand wave.

Afterwards, rocking silently in the boat, I experienced a kind of tunnel vision, as if I had been looking through the photographer's telephoto lens, which is how most of us experience wildlife these days. Now my field of vision was widening again to encompass the surrounding bay, the dome of sky, and our own strangely exultant faces.

When the whales surfaced again, they were far away, heading for the open sea. In the middle distance were the lights of our ship. We ran open throttle toward the ship, anxious to tell what we had seen. In the excitement, the brown bear had been forgotten, upstaged by a larger, seemingly more benign creature.

"Whales!" exclaimed the photographer. "How are you going to top that?"

Whales, however, were incidental to this cruise. The scientists aboard the *Alpha Helix* were conducting a survey of sea-otter feeding grounds in the Alexander Archipelago of southeastern Alaska. Sea otters are a keystone species, an animal that by its feeding and activities can modify the nature of the community in which it lives. Now, two days out of Sitka, we still hadn't spotted any sea otters. Mostly we had seen what sea otters eat: clams and sea urchins brought up by the divers in green net bags.

"We chase stores," said John Oliver, chief scientist aboard. "We know where the otter fronts are. We know where they're moving. Nobody's ever gotten in front of them to see what happens when they come into an area. We're getting in front of them just enough to see what happens when they move in and trash a place."

There was a certain irony in speaking of sea otters as trashing anything in the wake of the *Exxon Valdez,* when images of dead sea otters mired in oily goo, jaws caught in fatal rictus, "trashed" so to speak, had become the quasi-official measure of the spill's damage. But three months later, on the outer coast of Baranof Island, the spill seemed only a distant rumor of war. Prevailing currents had carried the oil slick westward from the grounded tanker and away from the Alexander Archipelago. The cruise plan of the *Alpha Helix* called for us to steam south to Dixon Entrance, not document atrocities in Prince William Sound. But the spill had forced many sea otters to migrate to new territories, presenting an opportunity to examine the effects of otter predation on previously undisturbed areas. We would be looking chiefly at their prey, marine invertebrates, creatures so small and arcane as to call into question where their lives even fit into the big picture.

The red Zodiac was the newest and fastest of the four small boats aboard the *Alpha Helix*. The only indication of John Oliver's rank as chief scientist on this cruise was that nobody else asked for the red boat. Oliver would ride figurehead in its prow, one knee on the rubber tube, hands clasped behind his back, except when he'd indicate a change in direction with a short chopping motion of his arm. We briefly crossed open coast, moving past wave-battered shoreline, scaring up gulls, until Oliver signalled us into a hidden bay on Beauchamp Island. Surfing on an incoming roller, we rode the wave through a gap in the rocks until they opened up into a cove, smooth and green in its depths.

Oliver spit into his mask and adjusted it so that the hood of his dry suit overlapped the top, leaving only an oval of exposed skin around his mouth. Then he tumbled backwards off the boat. Another diver followed, and I watched them disappear into a trail of bubbles.

These were "bounce" dives, a quick reconnaissance of areas likely to have clams or urchins. The dives would be marked on a map so that follow-up studies could be done in the future if sea otters moved into the area. Looking over the side, I could see, at a depth of twenty feet, what appeared to be rows of cabbage heads growing in sand. These were urchin barrens, barren of almost everything except sea urchins, which had grazed the algae and kelp down to bare sand and rock.

A few minutes later, Oliver hallooed from the far side of the cove, and I ran the Zodiac over to pick him up. He was holding a large fuchsia-colored sea urchin that resembled a hedgehog curled into a ball. ("Urchin" is French for "hedgehog.") After placing the urchin in a white collecting bucket, I hauled Oliver aboard, and grabbed my waterproof notebook to take dictation.

Oliver spit the words out.

"White sand bottom to fifty feet. Urchin barrens. Some sea pens. Sea cucumbers, some *Saxidomus* siphons, starfish—"

He was interrupted by the other diver, who surfaced holding an enormous *Pycnopedia helianthoides*, or sunflower starfish. It was mottled blue and gray, had more than twenty arms, and felt like wet papier maché. Before tossing the starfish back into the sea, Oliver placed it on his head and posed briefly as the Statue of Liberty.

In the evening, the scientists divided into groups to catalogue their data. One group classified species of clams in the dry lab; another entered dive logs into the two computers aboard. I joined a semi-circle of people who were sitting beneath floodlights on the aft deck and cutting open sea urchins. There was nothing rhapsodic about this aspect of field biology, except that it was the real work of the voyage. By comparing sizes and weights of these sea urchins with those in areas containing sea otters, the scientists hoped to learn about the effects of otter predation on prey communities. When otters move into an area, they decimate the sea urchins, which feed on kelp. The result is a kelp forest: an environment more suitable for fish than for shellfish. The implications of such research are important for places like the California coast, where a transplanted sea-otter population is frequently at odds with fishermen, as well as vulnerable to offshore oil development.

The urchins were piled in several white plastic buckets. They were red or purple, globular, and covered with articulating spines. They looked like something to hang on a Christmas tree. Like other echinoderms, such as starfish and sand dollars, sea urchins are marked by radial symmetry, their shells banded in swirls like Byzantium domes. Only the scratching of spines against the sides of the buckets reminded us that the urchins were alive.

Selecting a sea urchin, our leader, a doctoral student, would measure it across, weigh it, then split the shell with a diver's knife, letting the seawater drain out as if she were cracking an egg. Inside were orange fingers of roe (which taste like egg yolk), a watery gut, and an intricate, five-toothed jaw assembly called Aristotle's Lantern, used for grazing on kelp. After weighing the roe and guts on a tabular hanging scale, I'd call out the numbers, and then throw the whole mess over the side.

Someone had placed a boombox on the hatch cover. While *The Best of James Brown* blasted from the speakers, we shucked sea urchins at a rate even otters might find appalling. One of the crewmen, a droopy-pants character who called himself the Fishin' Magician, was jigging a line over the railing in the meantime. Pretty soon he caught something that bent his fishing rod into a parabola. A few of us stopped shucking urchins long enough to watch him winch a large red snapper over the railing. Workmanlike, the crewman yanked the hook out of the fish's jaw, baited up, and resumed jigging. By now we were all watching. The snapper was still alive, saucer eyes bulging, air bladder ballooning out of its mouth from having been brought up forty fathoms. Even the boombox couldn't drown out the awful flap of fish against deck.

"Why don't you put that fish out of its misery?" one of the grad students shouted. "Don't you know it's cruel to let something die like that?"

The crewman did a slow about-face. If he was intimidated by this circle of intent, questioning faces, people with advanced degrees, he didn't show it.

"Look who's talking. You guys just killed, what, a hundred sea urchins? At least I'm going to *eat* my fish."

Nobody had an answer for that, so the Fishin' Magician resumed fishing.

These days it's hard to know where one's sympathies should begin in regard to animals. "The question is not Can they *reason* nor Can they *talk*," Jeremy Bentham wrote a century ago, "but, Can they *suffer?*" Who knows what suffering means to an animal lacking a central nervous system? As a litmus test for where our loyalties to living organisms should begin, the capacity for suffering is as limited and anthropocentrically weighted as the ability to maintain eye contact. Bentham might as well have said, Can they *evoke* our sympathy? As far as echinoderms go, I don't think so. Still, under the floodlights, my hands, deep purple from shell pigment, suddenly looked bloodstained. As the feverish voice of James Brown launched into "I Break Out in a Cold Sweat," I couldn't help thinking of the next sea urchin.

On the third day of the voyage, the ship anchored in Aats Bay on Coronation Island. The photographer, her husband, and I took the gray Zodiac around the bay to look for sea otters, which were supposed to be in this area. The luxuriant brown kelp forests were a good indicator, as well as the small size of the few sea urchins the divers had found, living as fugitives in crevices under rocks, subsisting on drift algae.

A fog was burning off the water as we passed rafts of pigeon guillemots and pelagic cormorants. The first otters we saw turned out to be spotted seals arrayed like sunbathers on the rocks. They seemed naked and vulnerable and reluctant to return to the sea. Rounding the point to Alikula Bay, we finally spotted a sea otter, a female with a pup riding on her chest. She had a blunt, yellowish head, more catlike and clever looking than a seal's, and she never let the gap close between us. She whistled, and eight more otters popped up from a kelp bed where they'd been snoozing. Without taking their eyes off us, they moved away, back pedaling so that they appeared to be walking on water.

It's easy to see why people find sea otters so appealing. They look like furry hand puppets and obviously enjoy themselves. The history of their exploitation and near extinction is a familiar tale of human greed. It was the projected profits in sea-otter skins that prompted the United States to purchase Alaska in 1864, and the knowledge that the species was fast being depleted that made the Russians eager to sell. It's difficult to understand how people could have hunted sea otters so ruthlessly; for one thing, they had to get past those eyes.

After several days without sighting a whale, the photographer's husband, a cartoonist, began to grow listless. To entertain himself, he drew a cartoon strip on the mess-room blackboard entitled "What We Saw Today." There was a cartoon sea otter in a Mexican sombrero—"Otter Frajitas"—and a humpback whale breaching under John Oliver's rubber Zodiac.

"I'd be curious to know," said the cartoonist, "what you end up writing about. The whales were interesting, but otherwise this trip has been pretty dry—clams and bugs. What's the good of all this research? Frankly, who cares?"

The "bugs" were, in fact, nit-sized crustaceans called amphipods. Kathy Conlan, a biologist from the Canadian Museum of Nature, spent most of her time in the ship's dry lab, looking at them through a microscope. There are an estimated 25,000 species of amphipods in the world, only a third of which have been identified. Those on land are commonly called beach hoppers; those in the sea are scuds. The names are hardly promising. Kathy collected scuds with a bait trap lowered to the bottom and attached to a buoy. The trap was nothing but a screened funnel attached to a plastic jar baited with a dead herring. After an hour, she'd pull the trap up to find a nest of amphipods and nothing left of the herring but a fine comb of bones.

"Look at this," Kathy said. "Here's a female with a brood pouch of fifteen."

She was studying *Dulichia rhabdoplastis*, a species of amphipod that lives commensally on the spines of red sea urchins. Fastening a strand of detritus that trails off from the urchin's spine tip, the amphipod feeds on particles of plankton that float past. The sea urchin is the whole world to *Dulichia rhabdoplastis*, and it holds on for dear life.

Looking into the microscope, I felt like I was free-falling several rungs down the food chain. The spine of the sea urchin was magnified to the scale of a redwood, and balancing on it was a lobster-like creature with outsized claws and glowing, iridescent eyes. Hunched over her brood of young, mama amphipod moved with a hideous swaying motion. There is nothing spiritual in these lives, nothing exultant; they are simply grist for larger animals, from sea urchins to whales. In the waters off Coronation Island, the divers had discovered gouges in the soft mud of the sea floor made by gray whales feeding on amphipods.

"This one's a male," said Kathy, moving the specimen dish slightly until a larger amphipod hove into view. "You can tell it's a male because its claws are larger. They're not only used to defend territories but to grasp a mate as well. You can see he's holding a female under his thorax. They'll mate when the female molts. It's very exciting to watch!"

I climbed the stairs to the wheel house, which was dark except for the luminous green dials of radar and electronic navigation devices steering us through the night. We had left Coronation Island and were passing south of the lighthouse at Cape Decision (a flash every five seconds) toward Iphigenia Bay. The bay had been named by a nineteenth-century British naval officer to commemorate bad weather and his knowledge of the classics.

In Greek mythology, Iphigenia was the eldest daughter of Agamemnon and the first victim of the Trojan War. On the eve of

battle, Agamemnon's fleet lay stormbound. A soothsayer explained
the problem: the goddess Artemis had been offended because one
of Agamemnon's men had killed a sacred animal in the goddess's
sacred grove. (In some accounts the sacred beast is a stag, in others a pregnant hare.) To appease Artemis and get under way,
Agamemnon reluctantly agrees to sacrifice his daughter's life.

If Hollywood ever gets around to casting *The Sacrifice of Iphigenia*, the sacred grove would be Alaska, Exxon's CEO would play
Agamemnon, and the part of the sacred beast would be a toss-up
between a sea otter and a whale. Few creatures engage our emotions as intensely or elicit such outrage when threatened. Both are
marine mammals that have come back from the verge of extinction
to become flagships of the environmental movement. Both have at-
tracted the kind of merchandising once reserved for dead rock
stars: T-shirts, limited-edition commemorative coins, and, in the
case of humpbacks, record albums and hints of spiritual powers. If
an animal is a keystone species, does that necessarily give it more
spiritual significance?

The strategy of promoting highly visible species in order to protect entire ecosystems has been a successful one. It's been easier to
rally around "Save the Whales" than "Save the Oceans," even when
the oceans clearly need saving. But such a star system represents a
distorted view of life on Earth. Most of the species on this planet do
not have backbones. And it's the unruly masses at the bottom of the
food chain that support the big, glamorous mammals at the top,
not the other way around. Clams and sea urchins can get along perfectly well without sea otters, but the reverse is not true. We've sep-
arated questions of animal rights from those of habitat as though
the two weren't interconnected, as though the ocean itself weren't
a living organism. There is a kind of fatalism in all this, in narrow-
ing our focus to a few large mammals while smaller, inconspicuous
creatures, like the snail darter, slip toward the abyss. It's as if we
perceive the ark to be shrinking and believe that if only a few
species can be saved from extinction, they ought to be the sentient,

warm-blooded ones, the ones that remind us of ourselves. But the others, the smaller creatures we'd just as soon jettison, *are* the ark.

Head down, bent over, I made my way along the black shale beach of Thorne Island. It was a hot day. My orange float coat and rain pants lay in a heap on the beach. In the lagoon behind me, a scientist sunned himself aboard the Boston whaler, playing Irish tunes on a penny whistle.

Every so often I stooped to overturn a moist chunk of rock, flailing after the beach hoppers that skittered out from underneath and stuffing them in a plastic collecting bag. I had promised Kathy Conlan to look for terrestrial amphipods to add to her collection. I was chasing their stories, pretending to care, as she did, about the differences between species. But, in truth, their skittering only reminded me of cockroaches in past apartments I'd just as soon forget.

Moving up the beach, I found the bleached skull and ribs of a Sitka deer scattered among the luxuriant beach grass. Here was a mystery: What had killed the deer? Where was the rest of the skeleton? What was the story here? The poignancy of any skull is, of course, entirely a matter of how closely it resembles one's own. All morning I'd been walking on a boneyard of clamshells and cockleshells, a charnel house of ectoskeletons, unmoved because I could not imagine lives to inhabit them or stories for how those lives ended. Picking up the deer skull, I arranged it totemlike upon a rock, eye sockets facing out to sea.

The tide was ebbing. I waded out in my fireman boots to a rocky tide pool to see the lines of zonation, patterns of color on the rocks where one species' sphere of influence ends and another's begins. Starfish, which prey upon mussels, were the keystone species here. Clinging to the rockface like mountain climbers, they limit the downward expansion of mussels, while the height of the tide limits their own upward mobility.

A friend of mine who loves tide pools cannot bring herself to

climb over them because of all the small lives, almost indistinguishable from the rocks to which they adhere. It would be like
walking, she says, on people's heads. But I am no such saint and go
clambering over the acorn barnacles and mussel beds. We all live
in one tide pool or other and by the same harsh dynamics. We may
not chase after whales in small boats, harpoon in hand, but the
sheer weight of our lives is felt, and we must learn to place our feet
more carefully.

Starfish aside, I was for the moment the chief worry here, the
keystone species, the head honcho. Small crabs scuttled over the
rocks to hide in crevices, fleeing my approach as if I were the
biggest thing in the world, as big as a whale. Not one of them
paused to wonder whether my intentions were good.

Fables

The weather only worsened. The quick, lightning-shot storms of early summer were gone, replaced by a misting, wind-blown coastal weather that steadily ground me down. After the first hour at the throttle, I put on a wool sweater, then added a heavy woolen overshirt, a windbreaker, and finally a rubber rain poncho. Still, I felt chilled to the bone. A monotonous gloom settled over the day. The more I stared over the bow at the bobbing horizon, the less distinct it became—gray river, gray sky.

For a hundred and fifty miles below Kaltag, the Yukon flows through deserted country with no intervening villages and very few fish camps. It is a perfectly bleak terrain, a Euclidean landscape of bald headlands and muskeg swamps, all sharp right angles and planes. Across the river, the Kaiyuh Flats stretch in an unbroken line of alder and willow, while to the west a stark range of coastal hills soars above the river, their summits disappearing into the thick cloud ceiling.

The river was a mile and a half across, split into channels by wooded islands that went on so long I often mistook them for the shore. I kept to the leeward side and ran below the terraced banks, dodging in and out of the wind. Crossing an open stretch between islands, the canoe would buck in the whitecaps, climbing a green swell only to pitch forward when the bottom of the wave dropped out and drenched me with spray.

Late in the day, running in a light rain, I startled a flock of sandhill cranes on the point of an island. The birds nest in the Flats and were gathering now in large numbers to prepare for their autumnal migration south. A rush of gray wings, a few tentative hops, and the cranes went aloft with a great clangor. They flew across the river at a slight incline—long necks extended, legs trailing—breaking into three flights against the backlit sky. Then they headed back, circling to gain altitude. Higher and higher, the cranes kettled into the sky, a great wheel turning on the axis of the clouds.

Not being a naturalist, I'm interested more in my own species, but traveling through a long stretch of unpopulated wilderness I often wondered where all the game was hiding. Except for the occasional moose or black bear tramping along the beach, what wildlife I'd glimpsed on this journey had been in the sky above or the river below. These great migrations went on for the most part unseen. The birds and the salmon I did encounter always seemed to be in a crowd, always in a hurry, and always headed upriver. As the long summer days dwindled, I often got a sinking feeling that I was going in the wrong direction.

After ten hours at the throttle, I killed the engine and glided onto a sandbar, a tear-drop Atlantis recently emerged from the falling river. Without the outboard's constant droning, an immense silence settled on the water, broken only by the interior ticking of my own brain. I sat on a log in front of a driftwood fire, my heels dug into the sand, and watched the brown river steal past without a sound. In the west, beyond the headlands, a dull light was dying.

All day I had passed no other boats and seen no tents in the woods along shore. Only the land itself seemed alive—trees bend-ing in the wind, the fluid movement of the river—all part of a world that lives and breathes without men. In such a landscape, who wouldn't feel peripheral and alone? Perhaps to make the land less lonely, Natives had invested the natural world with spirits, believing that animals and even plants possessed something like a soul. Setting off on a hunt, a hunter might address his quarry in song so that his prey, when he encountered it, was more than a stranger. The soothing words also assuaged any lingering guilt he might have felt at stalking a fellow spirit. Even the animal's death was governed by ritual and social obligations. I remember a Yupik Eskimo from the delta, a bright student and natural leader, who grew unaccountably glum and anxious during his wife's first pregnancy. Later he explained that he had failed to share the first seal he had killed with the rest of the village, as was the custom, and so he'd been worried that if his wife bore a son, the boy would be physically marked by the father's transgression. His wife delivered a baby girl, as it turned out, so the matter was laid to rest.

I don't know how much currency that view of the world has in villages today, or how long such beliefs can withstand the onslaught of daily soap operas and satellite-beamed golf matches. It's easy to lament the passing of such traditions even though I cannot bring myself to believe that animals have spirits. If we were ever on speaking terms, we've long since forgotten the words or run out of things to say. When I've brought a deer down in the woods and crept up to finish the job, following the wounded animal's hemorrhagic breathing, the last thing I'd want to do is speak to it, or worse, have the deer speak back. Still, the tribal hunter rarely felt lonesome in the woods, which was how I felt at the moment. Marooned on this sandbar, I hungered for conversation, for contact with a soul other than my own.

Swimming out of sight, great schools of whitefish and salmon keep their own company in the river. Beluga whales sometimes lose their way in the labyrinthine channels of the Yukon Delta and stray far upstream searching for an outlet to the sea. The nineteenth-

century naturalist William Healy Dall mentions a white whale being killed a few miles below Nulato, at least four hundred miles
from saltwater, its appearance an ominous sign to the villagers of
something clearly out of place. But I think such a visitation would
be marvelous. Out on the river in the twilight, the canoeist feels
something rubbing against the hull as if he had run aground. Looking over the side, he sees a ghostly shape breach the surface, exhal-
ing mist from its blowhole. The head is pale and fetal, eyes set back
beneath the high, intelligent forehead, the mouth a droll curve.
Beluga and river traveler stare at each other across the vast evolu-
tionary gulf. In a high-pitched tremolo, the whale speaks. What it
asks is how to get home.

Through the rain, I saw a steam shovel, monstrous and wet, scoop-
ing gravel from the beach. The huge mechanical jaw hovered above
a dump truck as though about to devour it, then unclenched, emptying its load with a resounding crash so that the truck bounced
twice. I followed the dump truck up a puddled road past new frame
houses built on pads of gravel torn from the same beach.

Grayling was the only village I'd seen along the Yukon that did
not overlook the river. A half-mile back from the beach, it occupied
a flat tongue of land flanked by birch-covered hills. Behind some
trees, a helicopter was landing and taking off with a jet-age whine.
On the front porch of the Native Store several loose-limbed
teenagers stood out of the rain and looked me over.

Off the river, I was quickly reduced to the role of tramp, dependent upon the charity of others and, in bad weather, the shelter
of public buildings. So I went to mail a letter at the small post office. The mail plane had just landed, and the tiny foyer was jammed
with people. The postmistress stood on the other side of an open
dutch door dispensing mail. She wore an oversized cardigan
sweater and a crumpled man's hat, set cockeyed on her head, that
gave her a coquettish look. By the time I bought my stamps, everyone else had left.

"You look like you've been standing in the rain all day."

"More like three days," I told her.

The runoff from my rain poncho made a small puddle on the floor. I must have looked pathetic.

"Wanna come inside and warm up? I've got a stove in the next room. I'll put on some tea."

She held the dutch door open for me, then locked it shut. "So we won't be disturbed." From behind, the postmistress had a sweet, girlish figure, but her plucked eyebrows and smear of lipstick on her mouth made her look closer to forty. She'd made cozy quarters for herself adjacent to the mail room. There was a big potbellied stove and a television set blaring a game show. She'd decorated an entire wall of the room with pictures clipped from fashion magazines. Cover girls in various stages of cleavage and soft-focus lovers in fragrance advertisements stared down approvingly, although I imagined Grayling offered few opportunities to test out the wisdom of *Cosmopolitan*.

"Why don't you take off your wet clothes," she suggested, "and I'll get us something to eat."

She disappeared out the back door while, a little uneasily, I stripped off my rain suit and layers of wet wool, setting them beside the stove where they began to steam. Down to jeans and a T-shirt, I turned around to find the postmistress smiling at me. She'd returned with a loaf of spongy bread and a tin of cocktail sausages to eat with our tea. The room was already stifling, but the postmistress stoked the stove for my benefit until I felt flushed from the heat and the rose-scented cloud of her perfume.

Behind the stove was a wall map of Alaska. Tracing my finger down the Yukon River, I was perplexed at not being able to find Grayling on it.

"That's an old map," she said. "This place wasn't even a village until twenty years ago."

The people at Grayling had once lived far up the remote Innoko River at a place called Holikachuk. Since salmon didn't migrate up the Innoko, each summer the people would travel to the Yukon by way of an interconnecting slough to fish. In the early sixties, the BIA convinced the people to move permanently to Grayling where they would be less isolated. Now nobody was left at Holikachuk.

"I'll tell you something if you promise not to laugh," the post-mistress said huskily. "A long time ago, maybe a hundred years ago, people who were living way up the Innoko River killed a shaman. Before that shaman died, he told them that one day there would be no one living on the banks of the Innoko."

She pulled back a little. "Maybe you think that's a stupid story, but it's coming true! Nobody lives at Holikachuk anymore or at Iditarod or Flat. That leaves only Shageluk. And a lot of people are dying of cancer at Shageluk."

I didn't laugh.

"It's still pouring outside," she said, munching on a sausage. "Do you like games?"

After lunch, she brought out a Scrabble board. The television set still blared unwatched in the background.

"P-E-R-T," she said, spelling out each letter as she laid the little wooden tiles down on the board. "A triple word score. That's eighteen points!"

In no time at all, she was trouncing me. But then she came up with words I had never thought of before: hyphenated terms and misspellings and her own original compositions. But I didn't want to seem rude by pointing these out, especially since it was still raining.

While I tried forming a word on the board without vowels, a teenage boy came by (her son?) and gave me a hard-eyed look. When he left, I said I had to be going.

The postmistress pressed my knee warmly between hers.

"Are you married?"

"Yes," I lied. The funny thing was that I was a better flirt as a husband. A married man on the road is apt to act like a conventioneer, safe in the knowledge he has a home to go back to, while the single

man knows he has to lie in whatever bed he makes for himself. I
didn't want to wake up to any family scenes, besides being too
much a coward for this.

"Then maybe you can give me a little advice on married men,"
the postmistress said. "There's this helicopter pilot who's a real fox!"

I told her I was the last person to ask for romantic advice.
Putting on my damp clothes, I thanked her for lunch and headed
out to the rain.

She asked where I was headed next.

"Anvik."

She laughed. "That's a wild place! Two families got into
a shootout not too long ago in Anvik. They call it Dodge City!"

It was thirty miles by river to Anvik. The rain had stopped, but a
mist hung in tatters over the low mountains separating the Yukon
from Norton Sound.

The Anvik River came in from the west behind a long point of
land. I motored up the clear, dark tributary until I came to a village
sheltered in the lee of a wooded bluff. The small houses hanging on
the hillside and the damp smell of wood smoke made me think of
Appalachian hollows and feuding families locked in a deadly crossfire.

The Anvik general store had a plank floor and shelves stocked
with hardware and a few groceries. When I asked the manager
about the gun fight, he said the quarrel began over salmon stolen
from a fishwheel. He was young and blond, and I could see he
didn't want to talk about it.

"Things have quieted down since the shooting," he said. "One of
the people is in jail. Nobody got killed. Someone just took a little
buckshot in the hand is all."

He was less interested in Anvik's recent doings than in the safely
distant past. From the backroom he returned with a cardboard box
and set it on the counter. The box held a collection of Indian artifacts: milky blue trade beads from Siberia, bone awls and combs,

serrated ivory arrowheads, crescent-shaped slate ulus or women's knives, and a bear-tooth pendant.

The storekeeper had found these things across the Anvik River on a point where the old village had been. As the Yukon ate away at the riverbank, it exhumed old graves, spilling bones onto the beach, as well as possessions placed with the dead to sustain them in the afterlife. Just the other day the storekeeper had seen a coffin hanging over the river, ready to drop, and surmised a double burial since it held two small skulls. He was quick to point out that he never disturbed the bones that tumbled onto the beach, only the trinkets and tools buried with them. Otherwise they would be washed to the sea.

"I'm only keeping them temporarily," he said, "until the village gets around to building a proper museum."

He replaced the lid on the box.

"If you're really interested in the past," he added, "you ought to talk with my in-laws."

The storekeeper's wife made a telephone call, and a few minutes later her father came to fetch me. He was short and slight and walked with such economy of movement as to appear weightless. Joe Jerrou lived a short walk from the store in a frame house with sturdy, dark furniture and a needlepoint sampler on the wall. His wife Alta was waiting for us in the living room. She wore a high-collared blue print dress, sturdy black shoes, and rimless glasses. A tall and graceful woman, she was old enough to have grown up speaking Ingalik Athabascan and now taught it to children in the village school so the language wouldn't disappear entirely. She spoke with the slow solemnity of her years.

"There was a trail to St. Michael when people used to trade with the Eskimos for seal skins and seal oil for their lamps," she said. "The Indians always went to the coast in the spring when a crust covered the snow. They traded wolverine and wolf skin and 'made things' like wooden bowls and snowshoes. The Eskimos also liked the punk that grows on the sides of birch trees. Indians took baskets of it over, and the Eskimos mixed the punk with ashes to make a chewing tobacco."

The winter portage followed the Anvik River to its headwaters, then went over the divide to the Golsovia River and down the coast to St. Michael. It was the same route used by the Russian creole Andri Glazunov when he crossed from Norton Sound in 1834 to become the first white man to lay eyes on the Yukon River. The last time anyone from Anvik crossed the portage to trade with the Eskimos was in the late 1920s, although ten years before the route had been used regularly.

"The village used to be on a point across the river," Alta said, "until the mission built the church and the people started coming over. I attended the mission school but I didn't live in the boarding school because I lived right here in Anvik. The boarding school took in children from up and down the river, mostly orphans."

Joe Jerrou excused himself to get his hearing aid. When he returned, he recalled seeing the first plane to land in Anvik, a biplane that skidded onto the frozen river on skis and brought a precious cargo of smallpox serum.

"That was the first plane I ever saw. The pilot had to stay two days because a thaw made the ice too sticky for him to take off."

Two years before, Anvik had been hard hit by a devastating influenza epidemic. The outbreak came in late April while snow still lay on the ground and the Indians were preparing to leave for their spring camps.

"I was a little girl then," Alta recalled. "When the flu came, people scattered. Some of them made another village two miles below Anvik. Others just lived in the woods along the river. A lot of people died. They'd come down with the flu, then catch pneumonia, and die. Afterwards the mission school took in many orphans. In June a hospital boat came down, but by then it was too late."

The epidemic struck particularly hard at the elderly and those already weakened from tuberculosis. As many as four or five people died in a single day. Because the ground was still frozen and most of the men sick, coffins were heaped upon a scaffolding until graves could be dug.

"Doctor Chapman did the best he could with the medical supplies at the mission," Alta said. "But he wasn't an M.D. He was a doctor of divinity."

She was six years old when John W. Chapman left Anvik after a lifetime as its missionary. A picture of Chapman's son and successor hung on the Jerrou's living room wall. He was, she said fondly, the image of his father.

John Wight Chapman was a soft-spoken New Englander who had served his Episcopal diaconate in New York City before embarking for the Bering Sea under the direction of the Domestic and Foreign Missionary Society. On June 26, 1887, Chapman landed on the rain-drenched coast at the old Russian fort of St. Michael to begin his efforts. Walking on the beach a few days later, he chanced to see a squad of marines from the revenue cutter *Bear* escorting the shackled murderer of Bishop Seghers aboard. The Catholic missionary had been killed in his sleep by his lay assistant, now a baying lunatic. It was an inauspicious beginning.

Chapman and another missionary, Rev. Octavius Parker, purchased an old boat and hired a steamboat to tow them through the boggy delta and upriver to Anvik. Approaching the Ingalik village, Chapman saw old men sitting on the cutbank, hands drawn into their parka sleeves, watching impassively. "Something of a sense of loneliness came over me," he wrote, "as I landed among a strange people, who spoke or understood hardly a word of English."

"Ingalik" was a term given the Athabascan Indians of the lower Yukon by their Eskimo neighbors; it meant "louse-ridden." The Indians called themselves Deg Hit'an, or "the people from here." At the time of Chapman's arrival, they lived in underground hovels, relished spoiled fish eggs, and bathed in urine. They believed that when a man died his soul journeyed underground to a village of the dead located in the mountains at the source of the Yukon. Thus they regarded the pale strangers coming into their country as re-

incarnations of their deceased ancestors who had somehow lost
their way.

After the first winter in Anvik, Chapman and Parker moved the
mission across the Anvik River from the village to be more au-
tonomous. For thirty yards of ticking, fifty pounds of flour, and
some tea and sugar, they purchased land at the foot of Hawk Bluff.
Indian families were not allowed to live on mission land unless they
converted and paid a yearly rental of one dollar. The Anvik River
then became the dividing line between the "mission Indians" and
the unreconstructed, a wide Jordan between heathen and saved.

Parker departed the second summer, leaving Chapman on his
own. He stayed more than forty years. He built a church and a
boarding school but, despite the steady trickle of Indians across the
river to the mission, he felt himself losing the battle for souls with
the village shamans. How was he expected to compete with men
who conversed in dreams with animals or rescued the sun from being devoured by an eclipse?

To make his case, Chapman undertook to learn the Deg Hit'an
language. He found an extensive vocabulary that wedded the Indians to their country and particularly to the great river running
through it. To fix their position, for example, the Deg Hit'an chose
from a string of riverine adverbs corresponding to our cardinal directions. Thus, there was *ngido'* for "downriver," *ngine'* for "upriver," *nginiggi* for "back from the river," and *ngitthing* for "to the
river."

With the help of an Indian named Isaac Fisher, Chapman began
translating the legends and stories told in the *kashime,* or men's
house, to pass the long winter nights. It was not an easy task. He
wrote: "The one word which translates 'I thank thee' is an example
of Ten'a spelling. It is *hoxwoqourcrigudastcet.* A page of this writing has something unfamiliar about it at first." Chapman found in
the Deg Hit'an genesis a Creator specified only as someone being
above. The first of his creations was a porcupine, followed by a
white bear, a man, and a brown bear. Afterwards, the Creator re-

treated to a distant heaven from which he punished people for wrongdoing by taking away their food. A more vital character was Raven, who is called *Yoqgitsi* or "Your Grandfather." Always wandering and hungry, as well as oversexed, it is Raven who introduces confusion into the world and makes death permanent by blazing a trail for the dead to take so that they do not return in spirit form. Chapman may have searched in vain for moral equivalents to the Gospel, but what he preserved was the face of a culture he had dedicated his life to undoing.

A hazy sun had broken through the clouds when I left the Jerrous. Walking along the riverbank, I found the prim New England chapel with its white belfry and shake-covered walls that Chapman had built in a style to remind him of home. The mission boarding school next to it had fallen on harder times. The three-story building was painted chocolate brown, the windows boarded up, and a sign hanging over the door said Whitey's Cafe & Pool Hall.

At the store, I'd bought a copy of the folktales collected by Chapman and recently retranscribed by Deg Hit'an speakers, Alta Jerrou among them. Sitting beside the old church I read the book into the late afternoon. The stories were marvelous, full of humor and wisdom, with characters certainly truer to Indian life than the cruel savages of Jack London's fictions. They spoke of a life spent in the woods and on the river in a constant search for food. The plots were a curious blend of the mundane and the fantastic: a jealous wife who transforms herself into a brown bear to destroy her unfaithful husband, a lonely spinster who hears a singing fish and realizes too late it was a man, a mother's-boy who refuses to marry until he's forcibly "tickled"—a euphemism for rape—by two old hags called "the Dog Sisters." (Since men and beast share souls, characters change form as easily as slipping an animal skin over their own.) One story put me in mind of the box of relics at the store. A young girl who lives alone with her grandmother unearths a string of beads from an abandoned village. She brings it home to her grandmother who guesses where the beads came from and instructs the girl to return them. The next day the girl goes down to the river to fetch water and meets a man driving a big sled. She gives the beads back to the sled driver who turns out to be the ghost of her dead grandfather.

I thought of the stolen beads as I trolled slowly off the point of the old village looking for the exposed coffin the storekeeper had mentioned. But I never saw it. Perhaps the coffin had already tumbled into the river and begun a new journey.

Fences

I spent an afternoon tearing down a fence, three strands of rusty barbed wire strung between oak posts to keep cattle out of the orchard. I wore heavy leather gloves to coil the wire, which was brittle and kept breaking. One strand disappeared into a pine bole that had healed over it like an old wound, so I snipped the ends with a wire cutter and started a new roll. Dismantling the fence, like lowering a flag, signaled a shift in the land's meaning, namely that these ten acres were no longer an orchard but part of the lower pasture, a fact the cattle have known for some time.

Even without the fence, a border of pines remains to show that the hillside had been set aside for something special. Only a few apple trees are left, mostly wind-bent Greenings, to cast circles of shade in the afternoon heat. Now it's open ground covered by oxeye daisies, patches of white clover, and sunbaked cow pies. The orchard is my favorite place on the farm, maybe anywhere, because it's one of those half-wild places where the intentions of people and nature overlap, like an overgrown lilac hedge that marks a farm-

stead gone to woods. The land falls away to the west to overlook
Sheehan's cows grazing on the opposite hillside, their black-and-
white hides patterned like Mercator maps of the world. To the east,
along the section of fence I took down, there's a sunken lane running between the orchard and Night Pasture that Ed's cows walked
down every morning after being milked and then walked up again
every evening.

Apple trees were the blaze marks of civilization. Government
surveyors laying out Jefferson's grid upon the prairie often planted
apple seeds to mark the section lines, knowing the settlers to follow could distinguish an apple tree from a wild plum or a thorn apple. It wasn't the settlers themselves but the next generation who
planted orchards and ornamental shrubs around the farmhouse to
show that the break with wilderness was complete.

I can guess the varieties John O'Neill planted from a map of the
orchard that he sketched across two pages of a ledger sometime
around 1906, each tree marked by a pen scratch in columns as even
as figures on a balance sheet. The trees were a long-term investment, an act of faith that he and his descendants would be around
for some time to harvest the fruit of his labors. He favored Russian
varieties like Duchess of Oldenburg, Tetofsky, and Hibernal that
could survive a short growing season, but he also planted the Iowa
Beauty and the Wealthy, a variety developed by a Minnesotan who
crossed a cherry crab with the common apple. The orchard held a
dozen varieties in all to provide apples at different times of the year
and for different purposes. There were Duchesses and Patten
Greenings for cooking and pies, sweet Anisms for sauce, Whitney
Crabs and Longfields—a yellow apple with red stipples—for pick-
ling, Strawberry Crabs, which threshers called a harvest apple because it ripened early during threshing season, and finally the tart,
hard-skinned Wealthy to close out the season. Whether John
O'Neill drew his map after he finished planting or sketched it as a
blueprint of things to come I'm not sure, but the orchard was his
small-scale Eden, his clearest proof of order upon the land. When

it was done, he pressed a lady's slipper between the ledger's pages as if to remind himself of what had been replaced.

"Some of those old Patten Greening trees were twenty-five to thirty feet high. Ma always wanted perfect apples, so I'd climb the tree and throw them down to her through the branches. She'd catch them in her apron."

Ed and I are pulling fence posts. I slip a chain around the post, hooking it to the bucket on the Bobcat. Then Ed raises it up until the fence post dangles like a hanged man. The oldest are white oak, furry with lichen, cut from the surrounding land as it was cleared for the plow. We stack them by the salt block for firewood.

"We had an apple shed out here that was like an outhouse with bins. Ma would come down and sit and sort apples. Some night when it was going to get good and cold we'd haul apples into the basement. We had a hard red apple that wasn't any good till winter. About February they were damn good apples."

A farm with a lot of fences is one that recognizes different kinds of land and different possibilities for them. A fence announces our designs upon the landscape; it imposes limits. Before fence laws were enacted in the last century, farmers fenced their crops to keep them from being trampled by horses and cows and hogs. Cowboys may have sung "Don't Fence Me In," but certainly not anybody who had corn or wheat in the ground. The first fence laws coincided with the development of cheap barbed wire, so that livestock could be fenced in rather than out, and owners were liable for any damage their animals incurred while running at large. The state's current fence law defines "at large" as "to stroll, wander, rove, or ramble at will." Before that, it was every swine for itself.

The fence lines on this farm were laid out by an agent of the Soil Conservation Service during the thirties, when much of the northern plains was blowing away in dust storms. Civilian Conservation Corps crews in blue denim outfits and floppy hats fenced off the hollow, put marginal land in permanent pasture, and divided big, square fields into long, contour strips to follow the slope of the land. The field pattern was designed when the farm was more diversified and horses still did much of the labor. As machinery continues to get bigger, many farmers tear out fences to enlarge their fields until they resemble vast seas of soybeans or corn, undoing the conservation measures of an earlier generation. Ed has maintained most of his fence lines because they allow him to see the land in segments, to fine-tune it accordingly, even though the layout can seem daunting.

One day a man from the grain elevator in Stewartville came to spray the corn with herbicide. The sprayer was mounted on the back of his pickup with a fifty-foot boom that folded up like the wings of planes on aircraft carriers. He had never been here before and studied Ed's crop map as if it were a jigsaw puzzle. "I think we got enough to do her, but you never know. Depends on how the fields are laid out. Yesterday I sprayed for this woman down in Predmore. She had a lot of fields like this." He made a triangle with his hands. "I ran out six rows short of finishing."

A Depression-era attitude about money lingers on the farm, nothing being purchased new if something can be reused, so fence building often starts with a salvage operation. When the corral needed replacing, we began by tearing down an old sheep shed that anchored one corner of it. The shed was of indeterminate age, having been skidded to the site from a neighboring farm in the twenties. It had housed sheep, then hogs, and more recently a transient population of raccoons, along with lumber salvaged from St. Bridget's church hall. Built in the 1870s to house a local chapter of Father Matthew's Catholic Total Abstinence Union, the hall had waited thirty years for us to resurrect it as a corral. Some of the rough-sawn boards of yellow elm were thirty inches wide with no knots. Nails melted when we tried to hammer them into the boards, so we used spikes instead. When the new corral was finished we chainsawed the palings to a uniform height and burned the ends in a bonfire in the middle of the cow yard. Cows are immune to history and could care less if their corral once sheltered temperance meetings and church socials, but for us the fence is a reminder that nothing is lost forever. A tree becomes a shed, becomes a fence, becomes black smoke rising through tree branches into an everlasting sky.

Sometimes the farm is so cluttered with the past that a bonfire of old things seems refreshing. But if the past is inescapable, the future remains a distant cloudland of possibilities. Sharon spends a lot of time imagining different scenarios for the farm in the event it stops being one. Some days she favors a pick-your-own strawberry patch, other days a hardwood tree farm, a bed-and-breakfast, storage for boats and RVs, a riding stable—any ruse she can think of to keep it intact. All this seems so much pie in the sky. You only have to look at the houses being built across Highway 52 to see the future.

One miserably humid afternoon a car with Iowa plates rolls up the driveway and parks in the shade. The driver, a soft-spoken man wearing yellow-tinted shooting glasses, gets out to introduce himself. He's a businessman scouting locations for new Sporting Clays courses and likes the farm, he explains, because it's close enough to Rochester for members to get in a round of shooting after work. He's brought his wife and daughter along for the ride, but they remain in the car, immured against the heat.

Sporting Clays is the sport of simulated hunting, the man explains, something like golf with a shotgun. Shooters walk through a course laid out with different stations, where they shoot at clay pigeons thrown to duplicate the flight of a particular game animal. The sport originated in England but is gaining popularity in this country, combining as it does the American affection for firearms with our propensity for turning anything elemental into a competition.

"Do you know the first thing General Schwarzkopf did when he returned from the Gulf war?"

I did not.

"He shot a round of Sporting Clays."

A championship shooter himself, the man asks to look around, so Sharon agrees to give him a tour, beginning at the south end of the farm on an old township road that dead-ends in a canopy of oak trees. Leaving the car, we hike through the woods and over a cattle gate to the narrow end of the hollow. No cattle have been pastured here this summer, and the hollow is waist-deep in tall grass, blackberry brambles, and stinging nettles. The man bounds ahead, pointing out potential shooting stations, while his wife carries their little girl on her hip and swats deer flies tangling in her hair. The air is gelatinous and thrums with insects.

"It's not like trap or skeet," the man says, "because every station is different."

The shooting stations are often elevated like backyard gazebos and named for the quarry they are meant to suggest. For instance, at Springing Teal the clay targets are launched almost vertically to match the flight of teal off a pond; at Bolting Rabbit, the targets bounce along the ground like scared bunnies; and at Fenceline Quail, they snap up like a wild covey. All the shooter needs is a shotgun and a vivid imagination.

Near the spring, the ground turns squishy and sends up clouds of gnats. We hike up a cow path out of the hollow and into a cornfield, which the man announces would make a good site for the clubhouse and parking lot. He's still laying out stations, but I stop listening once I figure out that the course would sound like a small war. (Maybe that's what Schwarzkopf missed—the rattle of gunfire.) I had dreamed up any number of scenarios for what the farm might become, but here was an unimagined future—a happy hunting ground where shooters ride golf carts through the fields after work and blast away at imaginary creatures.

As we walk along the edge of the cornfield I nearly step on a tiger salamander. Striped yellow and black, the salamander is hunting earthworms in the exposed soil. The tip of its tail is missing, as if the salamander had been hunted recently itself. Despite this, it

doesn't spring or bolt or run away, but just lies there, a Stationary
Salamander, and no sport at all.

What wildlife exists on the farm thrives, for the most part, on the
edge of things, along the borders between fields and woods, between the cultivated and the wild. Fences bridge the gap between
one world and the other. Leave a fence long enough, and a line of
trees will grow along it. Like an ocean reef, a fence provides a
foothold for plants and animals that would not otherwise survive
the monoculture of cropland. The trees and bushes growing along
it furnish nesting and food for songbirds, cover for rabbits and
woodchucks, and a corridor for deer traveling from woods to cornfields. Ed tolerates the trees until their branches shade his crops or
threaten to knock him off his tractor; then he gets out the chain-
saw and cuts them back, because if he doesn't they'll eventually
take over. Cultivation is not a permanent state. A cornfield will revert to a meadow, but it never works the other way around.

When I rolled up the barbed wire that had enclosed the orchard,
I uncovered a linear prairie of weeds: gooseberries, purple vetch,
milkweed, Canadian thistle, wild mustard, catnip, Queen Anne's
lace, and wild grape—its twists and coils approximating the barbed
wire it had replaced. Some of these species are native but many are
not, such as cocklebur, which Ed never noticed until he combined
a neighbor's oats during the sixties and the seeds hitched a ride
back in the hopper. Eventually the cattle will graze or trample these
plants to get at the grass, but for a moment I had a glimpse of what
the land might have looked like before it was a farm and how it
might look again if we just walked away.

Pioneers were too busy plowing the prairie into furrows to take
inventory of what their moldboard plows turned over. If they noted
anything, it was usually the bowl of blue sky or how the wind rippled the grass into sea waves. One of the most evocative and de-
tailed accounts of the tallgrass prairie before it was plowed was

written by Henry David Thoreau, who traveled to Minnesota in 1861 on the longest and last journey of his life.

Thoreau was forty-three at the time, and slowly dying of tuberculosis, when a doctor advised him to "clear out" to a more salubrious climate and recommended the West Indies. But Thoreau decided to try the air out West. Then, as now, easterners came to Minnesota for their health; the new state had been shamelessly promoted as a health resort for consumptives. Thoreau left Concord in early May with a seventeen-year-old companion, Horace Mann, Jr., and traveled by train to Niagara Falls, Detroit, Chicago, and East Dubuque, Illinois, where they boarded the steamboat *Itasca* for the trip upriver. Because he was obliged to stop and rest frequently, the journey progressed more slowly and in greater comfort than Thoreau was accustomed to. As they steamed up the Mississippi River, he coughed incessantly and wrote in his journal, along with descriptions of bluffs and Indian wigwams, how the *Itasca* always whistled its approach to a town before striking its bell six times "funereally."

Disembarking at St. Paul, Thoreau and Mann carried their carpetbags, coats, and an umbrella to the American House, where they ate breakfast, then traveled nine miles by stage over the prairie in the rain. They settled into a hotel within sight of St. Anthony Falls and made daily excursions into the countryside to botanize. Thoreau's method with wildflowers was to stoop and pluck the blossom, vigorously inhaling its fragrance before pressing it into his plant book. He also carried a compass, a notebook, Gray's botanical guide, insect boxes, twine and cards, a dipper and water bottle, and several handkerchiefs. He made extensive lists of birds and flora, freely mixing common names with the Latin and sometimes guessing outright: "Here on the prairie I see the plantain, shepherd's purse, strawberry, violet sorrel (?), common red sorrel, *Ranunculus rhomboideus*, *Geum triflorum* (handsome), phlox (as on Nicollet Island), *Druba nemorosa*, with black pods, a scouring rush by a slough, low grass and sedge. But here the prairie is fed over by horses, cows, and pigs."

Two weeks later Thoreau and Mann took a small steamboat up the snaggy Minnesota River to the Lower Sioux Agency at Redwood Falls to witness the annual treaty payment to the tribe. They watched as "half-naked Indians performed a dance at the request of the Governor, for our amusement and their benefit," and Thoreau noted that buffalo were said to be twenty-five miles away. In an earlier journal, Thoreau copied down what the Swiss naturalist Edouard Desor had told him about the Indians' lack of names for wildflowers, "that they had a particular name for each species of tree (as the maple), but they had but one word for flowers. They did not distinguish the species of the last." In fact, the Sioux had many names for individual flowers, such as the pasque flower, which they called *hoksicekpa* and used for medicine, as opposed to flowers in general, or *wahca*. (On the trip, Mann gathered quantities of pasque flowers to send to his uncle, Nathaniel Hawthorne.) Through interpreters, Thoreau listened to speeches by the Sioux chiefs, including Little Crow, the most prominent, who, a year later, would lead his tribe in a bloody uprising that resulted in the death of four hundred settlers and the total negation of the Sioux's claim to the land. But by then Thoreau himself would be dead of tuberculosis.

What conversations Thoreau might have had with settlers in Minnesota can only be imagined, because he wrote so little about them except that their houses were set half a mile apart on the prairie and their fences were built of sawn boards. But in *Walden* there is a memorable scene in which Thoreau, off on a fishing trip, escapes a rain shower by taking shelter with an Irish farmer, his wife, several children, and assorted chickens. While rain drips through the roof, the Irishman explains how he makes a living "bogging" for a neighboring farmer, turning meadow with a spade for $10 an acre and the use of the land and manure for a year. When Thoreau, transcendentalist and Yankee bachelor, regales the family with his own experiments in thrift, telling the poor bog-trotters that if they only worked less they wouldn't be inclined to eat so much, he sounds like a college kid home from the commune. "If he and his family would live simply, they might all go a-huckleberrying in the summer for their amusement." The Irishman heaves a sigh, and when the shower moves on so does Thoreau.

We've all gone a-huckleberrying of late, though our lives are hardly simple. Every schoolboy knows that the worst way to make a living is by physical labor. Leisure has been turned into an industry that even Thoreau would find unrecognizable, and the places we hold in highest regard are the scenes of our vacations, not our workaday lives. This public affection for wilderness often seems a way of pretending not to notice the wholesale destruction of our cities and countryside. If *Walden* remains a disturbing book, it is because the author advocates preserving the wild not by setting aside a few roadless parcels of land but by incorporating it into one's own life.

So I was interested when I heard that a pair of doctors who had bought an old farmstead between St. Charles and Chatfield were restoring part of it to tallgrass prairie. True prairie is made up of three-hundred-plus plant species, some of which have been lost forever, so a restored prairie is essentially a landscape of imagination. Recreating a prairie ecosystem on a few acres of unmowed pasture may be no more possible than bringing back the herds of buffalo, but it's a landscape I wanted to see, and imagination didn't seem a bad place to start. "To make a prairie," wrote Emily Dickinson, a stay-at-home who certainly never saw one, "it takes a clover and one bee."

> One clover, and a bee,
> And revery.
> The revery alone will do,
> If bees are few.

Steve Henke and Nancy Peltola are family physicians who work in St. Charles and Chatfield, respectively, and bought their farm ten years ago because it lay equidistant from their separate practices.

Henke gave me directions over the phone, explaining that if I passed the Amish school I'd gone too far. The Amish farms are easy to spot. There are always workhorses in the field, and no satellite dish. On the porch of one farmhouse I passed, an old woman was laying out quilts, her chalky face framed inside a black bonnet like water at the bottom of a well.

Overshooting my turn, I circle around at the one-room school-house and backtrack to find the doctors' farmhouse at the end of an unmarked gravel road—and nobody at home. I hike up a grassy ridge past a windmill and a ruined cistern. The ridge is bright and windblown as it curves above the valley and the white road I came in on. At the end of the ridge, in the heat-wavering distance, two people stand in a swarm of horses.

Nancy Peltola sits in the spring seat of an ancient Farmall-M while her husband unrolls a spool of fence wire from a wagon hitched to the back of the tractor. They are stringing a new paddock for their horses, who drift around us like smoke. A fawn-colored foal keeps inserting her muzzle between us, and the mare doesn't mind; but when a sorrel gelding gets too close, she kicks him in the ribs.

Of the hundred acres the doctors own, roughly half are tillable and have been rented to a neighboring farmer; the rest is ridgetop and impossible slopes, a kingdom of sunlight and wind. The farm-house had stood empty for years when the doctors moved into it. Friends suggested they bulldoze and start fresh, but they gutted the walls and rebuilt the house along its original lines. Not long after the renovation, a man came to the door and announced that he had been born in the back bedroom in 1927. His grandfather had built the house, and the man was surprised to find it still standing. Walk-ing past freshly painted walls, he followed his memory to the scene of his birth and found, instead, a music room. Now the doctors are restoring the landscape along its original lines, burning hillsides in springtime and sowing the seeds of prairie forbs and grasses so that at least some of the land will remember its past.

"Before we came here we didn't know anything about prairies," says Steve Henke. "We were mostly interested in woods. If you asked Nancy or me ten years ago if we'd want to live in a place with few trees, we'd have said no."

Trees are the death of prairie, the climactic stage in a biological succession that in the wild was circumvented by drought and fire. True prairie has only one tree per acre. The only prominent trees in view here are a stand of Norway pines, the remnants of a wind-break behind the farmhouse. The doctors had planted maples along the south end of the ridge to provide cover for wildlife, but the saplings succumbed to last summer's drought and now poke leafless and wandlike from the grass.

While Nancy walks back to the house to fix lunch, Steve gives me a tour of the back side of the ridge. The terrain is dry and rolling, covered with only a thin layer of sandy topsoil, a good place for a prairie remnant to have escaped the plow. Steve stoops beside a fernlike clump of silvery green leaves. "These are leadplants. And when you see leadplant, it's a pretty good indication the land has never been tilled. Once its seedbed is disturbed, leadplant doesn't do very well."

It's hard to tell the native plants from the aliens, and the most pristine meadow of wildflowers may prove to be a gathering of im-migrants. Steve points out the lupinelike blossoms of a prairie turnip, which is native, and yellow goatsbeard, or prairie dande-lion, which isn't but performs the neat trick of closing its petals at midday like a long wink. He finds a pasque flower past its bloom. This was the first prairie forb he learned by sight and name, and it sparked his interest in the restoration project. One morning dur-ing their first spring in the farmhouse, Steve and Nancy looked out of a window and saw scraps of white paper littering their hillside. Taking a break from remodeling, they climbed the ridge slope to discover that the pale scraps were hundreds of pasque flowers in bloom. Last year they harvested one-third of a pound of pasque flower seeds to trade at Prairie Moon Nursery outside Winona for prairie seeds they didn't have. The mixture of wildflower and grass seed had been gathered from virgin prairie farther north, near the town of Fertile.

Steve wears sandals, white running shorts, and a big straw hat. When the wind ruffles the brim of his hat, it reveals a red bandanna knotted pirate style around a receding hairline. Wandering through the tall grass along the ridge, he tosses names over his shoulder as if introducing guests at a dinner party. "This is pussy toes . . . buffalo pea . . . harebell . . . wild rose. . . . Here's one of my favorites, prairie smoke. It looks like a puff of smoke. . . . This is . . . nope. That's wrong. We'll have to look that up in the book at home. . . . You know what this is, don't you?" He gestures toward a particularly lush, three-leafed plant growing by a sandstone outcropping. "Poison ivy."

Certainly the first act of restoration must be memorizing the individual names of flowers and grasses that would otherwise blur under the general heading of "weed." In Genesis, naming is Adam's only task in creation, and it seems a measly chore, the one we give children when we bring home a pet; except that without names there can be no personal connection, and there is no love in the abstract. The common names for plants—like "prairie smoke" for *Geum triflorum,* for instance—are memorable precisely because they're metaphoric, nicknames based upon prior associations rather than the cold logic of Linnaean taxonomy. They are terms of familiarity, and walking through a meadow calling the plants by name is like entering a room of friends instead of strangers.

When he comes across a spiny-leafed plant bowing under the weight of a purple flower head, Steve hacks off the stem with the heel of his sandal. He does the same thing to the next one, and the next. "If you don't control them, they'll take over a field. There's an Amish man down the road, and half his pasture is thistles. Even a goat won't eat them."

The Canadian thistle is an ornamental accidentally introduced from Europe when it was mixed with crop seed and quickly got a foothold in overgrazed fields. Like many native prairie plants, it's a perennial that can propagate not only by seeds from its purple flower head but also by its creeping root stock, or rhizomes, so that new shoots will soon replace the ones Steve has hacked off.

"The true management of thistles is pasture management. They like disturbed soil, so if you don't let your animals crop the pasture too low, they can't get a start."

In May, Steve and Nancy bought six bred Holstein heifers, which they plan to sell in September. The cows are summer guests and represent a paradigm shift in the doctors' original notion that the prairie could simply restore itself. The cattle are stand-ins for the wild herds that once grazed here.

"When this was tallgrass prairie, it didn't sit idle. There were animals and burns. We learned that for the health of the land it has to be grazed. There was a man down in Iowa trying to rejuvenate prairie, and he wasn't having much luck until he borrowed a neighbor's herd of cattle. It sure speeded up the process."

Buffalo kept the prairie grasses green by feeding on their competitors, by fertilizing the soil with their manure, and by preparing a seedbed as they tore up the thatch with their hooves. Domestic cattle do all those things, but they do them to excess. Buffalo herds ranged across the open landscape like the weather itself, but the livestock that replaced them were confined by fences into smaller and smaller quarters and eventually grazed the prairie to death. The doctors' solution to that problem is more fencing. Using lightweight Polywire, they strung a grid of eight paddocks across their pasture and moved their Holsteins to a different paddock every three or four days. Rotational grazing imitates the effects of migratory herds without the complications of loosing buffalo among the cornfields.

We climb a barbed-wire fence into a grassy swale that looks like a neglected meadow except for the intense, pointillistic green blades rising among the brown tangle of weeds. This is a mesic prairie, midway between dry and wet, better suited to native grasses than wild forbs, so there is less phlox and bergamot but more porcupine grass and clumps of little and big bluestem. We watch wind currents moving through the grassheads on the far hillside like waves of light. A bobolink flutters overhead, singing like a hysterical music box.

"This is the area we burned last summer. We did roughly twelve acres. Two weeks later you couldn't tell it had ever been burned."

Prairie restorationists use controlled burns to set back the cool-season grasses introduced by Europeans—timothy, bromegrass, and orchard grass—so there's less competition for native hot-season grasses like big and little bluestem. Unless it is disturbed by periodic fires or grazing, the accumulated thatch grows so thick that the prairie eventually suffocates much of its variety or is invaded by forest. Fire does no permanent damage to the prairie plants, whose underground root systems resemble the tributaries of a great river system and allow the plants to conserve moisture, making them virtually immune to drought or fire. It was the constant growth and decay of these roots that formed the rich, chernozem soils of what would eventually become the corn belt. The thickly woven mat of roots was so interlaced that it broke the pioneers' wooden plows and awaited the development of John Deere's steel moldboard plow.

Indians set the prairie afire for a variety of reasons. A wall of flames was useful for driving game, eluding enemies, greening up horse pastures, or just cutting down on summer insects. The fires were great natural spectacles. A Methodist circuit rider described one such encounter in 1835: "The last twelve miles we traveled after sundown & by firelight over the Prairie, it being on fire. This was the grandest scene I ever saw, the wind blew a gale all day, the grass was dry. . . . In *high* grass, it sometimes burns 30 feet high, if driven by fierce winds. By light of this fire, we could read fine print for ½ a mile or more." Of course, the spectacle could prove fatal if the observer was caught without a swift horse. One writer advised settlers to light a backfire to delay the inferno's advance, then "ride madly before the wind." If that failed, the settler could always disembowel his horse and climb into the cavity until the flames passed.

Maybe what the countryside needs is a good conflagration now and then to cleanse it, an annual rite of purification by which we torch the old growth and then "ride madly before the wind." Afterward we'd return to find the land uncluttered again, and could sustain for a little longer our belief in its endless possibilities. Not a bad idea. We'd get to see the landscape as the Sioux or Thoreau did, its wide-open horizons the perfect screen on which to project our daydreams. The only catch is that we'd have to be willing to travel light, nothing more than could fit onto a travois or a prairie schooner. Not long ago, one of the immense new houses south of Highway 52 caught fire when a rag soaked in paint thinner ignited spontaneously in the garage. The blaze spread quickly and the house burned to the ground; but it must have had tough rhizomes, or good insurance, because a few months later it had grown back, bigger than ever, squatting on the hillside and ugly as a toad.

When Steve and Nancy burned their twelve-acre swale, they could have jumped over the flames. The Minnesota Department of Natural Resources, which issued the permit, stipulated that the winds on the day of the fire should not exceed five to ten miles an hour, or the humidity be less than 50 percent. The permit was issued for the first Saturday of the month—May Day, as it turned out. A crew of friends used torches dipped in a mixture of gasoline and diesel fuel to ignite the north end of the swale so the fire would burn against the slight breeze. The flames may have been small, but the green prairie grasses sent up a billowing screen of smoke. Sparrows and meadowlarks shot ahead of the blaze. The crew, carrying five-gallon piss packs, contained the fire except when sparks from an old cedar fence post ignited the edge of a nearby field and the flames had to be swatted out with rakes and brooms. A neighboring farmer, drawn by the smoke, came up to watch the doctors burning their prairie. "Oh," he said dryly, "I see you're making a clearing for thistles."

When sons-in-law get itchy to drive your tractors, you put them to work repairing fences because it's nearly impossible to wreck a posthole digger. I spend the morning straightening metal T-posts on a section of fence over east, staggering them with pressure-treated wooden posts that the frost can't heave. Unless I feel like chipping through limestone, it's necessary to find the old post-holes. The digging is tolerable where the fence line dips into shade, but in open ground the sun beats down like a hammer. I roll barbed wire off a spool in the bed of the pickup and, after it's secured at one end, use a fence tightener to pull it taut. A good fence is horse-high, hog-tight, and bull-strong. It's also a way of keeping faith that the land will remain a working farm.

Driving past the old orchard, I stop to pick a prairie bouquet for Sharon: bergamot, oxeye daisies, wild phlox, Queen Anne's lace. The cows haven't cropped the grass along the fence line yet, and I wonder what her grandfather would think of his bare hillside now or how he'd feel if it was diced into view lots or restored to tallgrass prairie. Either way, a kind of betrayal.

Exile's Song

Genealogy once struck me as a morbid hobby, a form of ancestor worship in which the living connect themselves to the dead through flow charts as elaborate as electrical circuitry. But climbing the family tree can provide a larger context for one's own life; it's a *momento mori*, in other words, and a bit of a detective game. I'd become interested in Catherine Esmond, my wife's great-grandmother, in the course of writing a book about the family farm. In 1852 when she was sixteen, Catherine emigrated from Ireland to Philadelphia where she worked as a maid. The Irish servant girl was a stock figure of the times though undoubtedly it was an easier life for a single woman than the mills. Eventually, Catherine married a dairy farmer, another Irish emigrant, who moved them even farther west, to a prairie farm in Minnesota. She lived to a "great age," as they say, and was a looming presence in my father-in-law's childhood, an old woman in widow's weeds who carried a cane she called her "gad" and shook it at grandchildren who didn't move out of her way fast enough. A gilt-framed photograph moldering in the farmhouse basement shows a middle-aged Catherine wearing a broach with a Celtic cross at her neck. Even in sepia tones, you can tell that her hair was bright red and her eyes a chilly shade of blue. Searching those eyes, you hear—or think you ought to hear—time's own sad music.

But by the time I started looking nobody could recall the Irish village Catherine Esmond had turned her back on or why she'd left. We knew the end of that life, but not its beginnings, and, while she wasn't my kin, her steerage passage from here to there had been an ordeal shared by an entire generation of Irish emigrants, my own distant relations included.

The genealogist's dream is of opening a steamer trunk to find, among the deceased's possessions, a leather-bound diary embossed "My Life and Obscure Times." Instead, ordinary lives are reconstructed from such fragments as death certificates and census reports, obituaries and probate records. After spooling through miles of microfilm of Griffith's Valuation, a nineteenth-century Irish tax roll, I'd located a handful of Esmonds in County Wexford. I wrote the parish priest in Balleygarrett, requesting him to check church records, and tucked a small donation in the envelope. A month later, the priest wrote back to say that he thought we had a match. Six months later, my wife and I flew to Ireland. We were acting out the exile's dream of coming home rich. Besides, I wanted to see if anything I'd written about Catherine Esmond's childhood was true.

Balleygarrett is a bump on the coast road south of Dublin—two pubs, a grocery, and a church. Our Lady Star of the Sea is a gray Victorian with an impressive belfry soaring above the level farmland. Inside, the church was boxy and cold. My wife and I lit votive candles then sat in a hard-backed pew courting our souls until the spell was broken when a family shuffled in for a baptism, carrying an infant heaped with white linen. They crushed noisily into the forward pews, clothes smelling of peat smoke and damp. Above the altar, a stained glass window depicted the Blessed Virgin Mary as a young woman trampling a snake underfoot. Her milky skin, thin lips, and long-suffering face mirrored half the women in the baptismal party. Mirrored my wife as well.

After the baptism, we sat in the rectory parlor while Father Byrne traced his finger down a column in the old parish registry. The names were scrawled in Latin and indecipherable in places but one was unmistakable. *Catharina Esmond,* baptized the day of her birth, December 19, 1834, to *Johnnis Esmond and Brigit Kavangh of Killenagh.* An entry, three years later, marked Brigit's death, followed, after a decent interval, by the remarriage of her widowed husband to a woman who bore him a steady stream of sons. Not many facts on which to hang a narrative. Still, it's not difficult to imagine young Catherine's position eroding as she became the unpaid servant to her half-brothers. The sheer volume of entries in the registry was even more revealing.

"Eleven weddings in the month of February," the priest remarked. "Now you wouldn't have that many in a year."

The parish population had dropped over the intervening years from six thousand (including Protestants) to less than a thousand, many of whom were seasonal residents as the countryside undergoes a transition, in the priest's words, from agriculture to "holiday homes for Dublin people."

The great divide of Irish history is, of course, the Potato Famine, separating as it does a population bursting at the seams with one whose sharp decline made possible the green and empty landscape of the Irish Tourist Board, that dreamy land of memory and subject of a thousand sentimental ballads. The blight, *phythopthera infestans,* that destroyed four successive potato crops occurred throughout Europe but resulted in famine only in Ireland, where a rickety pyramid of debt stretching from landlord to peasant had left the latter almost entirely dependent upon the potato for sustenance. The failure of the potato crop raised food prices beyond the means of the poor, and extreme hunger, combined with abnormally cold winters, led to dysentery, typhus, and cholera. At least one million Irish died during the Famine, and for every corpse laid in the ground, two more chose to emigrate. One of these was sixteen-year-old Catherine Esmond.

The village of Killenagh, a few miles north of Balleygarrett, had seven hundred inhabitants the year of Catherine's birth, according to *A Topographical Dictionary of Ireland* (1837), which also noted that the land was "almost exclusively under tillage." During the Potato Famine, outright starvation wasn't as widespread in County Wexford, with its barley fields and herring fishery, as in the west of Ireland, but as food prices rose everywhere, the poor fell into arrears on their rent, and evictions allowed landlords to consolidate their holdings, converting a patchwork of cultivated fields into more profitable grazing land for livestock. Today Killenagh is mostly pasturage, stone walls, and scattered farmhouses. What remains of the village is a thatch-roofed pub at the crossroads where we asked directions to the Porter farm. Griffith's Valuation showed the Porters owning the largest farm in the townland. Apparently, they still do.

Howard Porter was loading round bales on a blue Ford tractor as we pulled into his courtyard. He had red hair, muddy boots, and moved with the alacrity of a man who punched his own time clock. When I explained that we were looking for the old Esmond place, he dashed into the farmhouse. He returned with an ordinance survey map of the district and unrolled it on the roof of our rental car. The map showed land divided not in the orderly rectangles of a Midwestern grid but the helter-skelter logic of a dried-up lakebed.

"This land here belonged to them. Five acres. A long field. My father always called it Esmond's Turn Field."

"Really?" I asked. "Why is that?"

Porter gave me a funny look. "Because it's on the *turn* of the road!"

The Esmonds had owned five acres, a fairly typical holding in the last century for Catholics, who tended to divide their land evenly among sons, while Protestants, like the Porters, kept theirs intact by the practice of primogeniture. (None of this could have meant much to a girl like Catherine.) The Esmond "farm" had long since been swallowed up in one of their more prosperous neighbor's pastures.

Howard Porter led us down the road at a brisk pace to where it turned; then he climbed a thorny hedgerow to point out the field in question. There was standing water in the pasture and grazing sheep. The stone walls that had once defined the Esmond place were gone, but a pair of lofty oaks showed where the boundaries had stood.

"See where the little house must have been, that hump at the end of the field? It was gone when I was a child. My father plowed it up and used the flagstones for the hedgerows."

So we were standing on the remains of the Esmonds' ancestral home. Catherine's father had been a carpenter but probably kept a lazy bed of potatoes and a boat at the shore for fishing. A little effort and you could imagine a whitewashed cottage, a pig rooting in dung, the velvety leaves of the potato plants that looked, at the blight's onset, as if they'd been dipped in tar. The noxious odor of decay—the smell of famine! Or maybe not. Finally, there was only this damp field, sheep grazing in the middle distance, the dark bulge of the Wicklow Mountains, and beyond that the wide world.

On the way back to the car, my wife mentioned that her family, the Esmonds' descendants, still runs a farm in Minnesota, 240 acres, a modest operation by Midwestern standards but a veritable Ponderosa to an Irish farmer.

"They were lucky to get out," Porter said as he jogged back to his tractor. "The land here is too wet. Too mooky."

Some of those who stayed behind are buried down the road in an old cemetery at Donaghmore. The tilting limestone slabs and Celtic crosses are surrounded by a low stone wall with a breezy view of the Irish Sea, and, except for a nearby caravan park, the dead have it all to themselves. The ground was soft and hummocky and a constant reminder that you were tramping on someone's bones.

We searched in vain among the tombstones for Catherine's mother, dead at the age of twenty-five, but the place was fairly stuffed with Kavanaghs, some of whom might have been kin, so I wrote down their names. *"Here lieth the Body of.... Depd this world...."* was the standard inscription, flanked by radiant suns and other emblems of hope. Catherine had escaped their particular fate by crossing this very sea to Liverpool, then sailing on a larger ship to America, where she hoped to reinvent herself.

A coastline makes for dramatic departures, and Ireland is mostly coast. Leaning over the ship's railing, the emigrant takes a picture in her head of the fast-receding shoreline of home. Many emigrant ballads contain exactly this image of sad parting, with its dark undertones of banishment and hints at a glorious return. During the Civil War, Catherine spent off-hours in her maid's room, filling a scrapbook with newspaper accounts of Irish-American regiments, like New York's 37th Regiment, the Irish Rifles. Among the lithographs of General McClellan and exiled Fenian leaders, she pasted a poem entitled "The Downfall of England," delivered to "loud cheers" before the Brotherhood of St. Patrick, which concludes:

> *Unite and by the famine graves,*
> *By your sires' sacred dust,*
> *You shall not, will not, long be slaves ...*
> *The time is nigh—arouse! awake!*
> *For Ireland's sake unite.*

Yet few emigrants bought a return ticket, even after the famine ended. Instead, they fashioned a new life abroad and continued to see themselves as exiles, substituting an Ireland of memory, that misty isle for which tenors perpetually pined. A strange penance for leaving home. Catherine never went back. Her bones lie in a Minnesota cemetery, where the view, filtered through a shelterbelt, is of cornfields.

In the west of Ireland, the towns sound like birdsong: Kil-rush! Kil-kee! Tra-lee! We were staying in a friend's stone cottage in County Clare with its bare headlands and heartbreaking cliffs. The friend had predicted "soft" weather for March, but the wind blew a steady gale. At night we heaped the bed with quilts and fell asleep to cows bellowing in the adjoining stable. During the day, we drove the country roads.

Stormlight—the sun tunneling through clouds. At every farmhouse a skulking dog and round hay-bales wrapped in black plastic. Tatters of the wrapping hung on fences and thrashed in the wind like black pennants. The roads themselves were puddled and narrow, stone walls hidden under blackthorn and gorse, and driven by locals with an abandon that one might call Irish fatalism. Nobody, I'm told, walks away from a car accident here. Every time I hit another pothole, my wife sang out "Got it!"—as if there'd been a choice.

Road construction had been the principle activity of the relief works during the Famine to keep the hungry from inundating work houses. When the poor showed up, they were put to work building roads, often leading nowhere, largely because of the British government's infatuation with laissez-faire, its cool reluctance to give something for nothing—even charity. Many of the starving wretches died on their way back to the work houses. The roads are their revenge.

The West of Ireland never fully recovered from its depopulation in the nineteenth century, which is why the countryside is so empty and beautiful. Stone cottages open to the sky dot the landscape. Sometimes these are resurrected as dairy barns—a herd of Fresians hock-deep in the old kitchen. The industrialization of agriculture has been slower here than in the United States though its effects are the same: bigger tractors but fewer farmers. (Tourists may soon find the abandoned farmsteads of Minnesota as picturesque as those of County Clare.) I noticed it was always the ruins we stopped to photograph, never the places where people actually lived, perhaps because their stories weren't so obvious.

The Irish government has begun resettling families from the slums of Dublin in the rural west to reverse its depopulation even though there aren't necessarily jobs for them. One night the farmer who rents the muddy pasture behind our cottage stopped by and helped me light a peat fire in the hearth. We talked over tea about farming though I could barely understand him through the dense fog of his west Clare accent. He didn't speak Gaelic, but enough of its inquiring cadences survived so that he seemed to inhale his words after briefly letting them out. He was keeping close watch on a mare due to deliver in a month. She'd had her first foal last year, but it developed scours and died in a few days, leaving his daughter heartbroken. "Hardest thing I ever had to do was to bury that foal."

The farmer didn't much care for the resettlement families down the road. "They don't work. I don't think they know how." His own family had resettled themselves abroad: brothers in England, a sister in the Bronx. (A visit to the latter had confirmed his view of America as an endless TV cop show.) After boom times in the 1980's, Ireland has slumped back to double-digit unemployment, and nearly everyone has family living elsewhere on the globe, not just in the usual enclaves of Boston or New York but also in Tokyo and Singapore. So the diaspora continues. Half of Ireland's population is under twenty-five and face the old question of whether to stay or leave. Like Catherine Esmond, they understand that geography needn't be fate.

On St. Patrick's Day, we drove into town for the parade. Kilkee is a weekend destination for Protestants from Limerick, a seaside resort on the English model with a horseshoe-shaped strand and promenade of Victorian row houses. This was only its second attempt at extending the season with an American-style parade, but the weather wasn't cooperating. The FunFair and Leisure Centre were shuttered; the beach wave-tossed and deserted. The wind blew straight off the Atlantic, all the way from America, so fiercely that it snapped banners and sent children's caps twirling down the street. The parade came around twice, so it seemed longer than it really was. Tractors pulling floats—a boxing club, a troop of Brownies from Kilrush, a rescue squad riding a rubber dinghy. None of the floats seemed particularly nationalistic and only one commemorated the past, in this case the evictions of the nineteenth century. ("In April 1848, Captain Kennedy calculated that 1,000 houses had been leveled since November.") The float carried two men dressed as Keystone Kops who swung a log mounted on a tripod against the door of a cardboard shanty; every time the door opened, out flew a pailful of water. History as burlesque.

In America, St. Patrick's Day is a memory binge, and the memories, now third- and fourth-hand, are more about the idea of a country than any actual place. Both of my grandfathers were sons of emigrants, and at family gatherings would put on stage accents and call each other "Murphy" and "Schultz." Otherwise, they had no use for the past . . . except perhaps at the end. In a nursing home, the "Murphy" grandfather was an occasional time traveler, recalling his own distant childhood in starts and stops. His family had maintained their emotional bonds to Ireland in the usual ways: the Church, membership in the Ancient Order of Hibernians, and syrupy ballads of exile sung at an upright piano. His father came from Donegal, and like most Irish emigrants who'd fled the countryside, he settled in a city. The only photograph I recall showed him surrounded by children on a shady Chicago porch, a heavyset man with a cocked bowler and handlebar mustache and the face of a mean butcher.

At the dance that night in Lynch's Pub, a local band called The Oyster Boys played country-western music for their first set. A couple in black cowboy hat and jeans line-danced among the two-steppers. After the break, the band switched to traditional Irish songs, but the lyrics were the same litany of lost loves and dead-end jobs.

My wife whispered, "Every face I remember from childhood is in this room."

It was true. Irish-Americans cannot visit Ireland without thinking they've found the headwaters of that great gene pool of sad blue eyes and malicious grins. In high school I was taught by Irish Christian Brothers and had come to think of a brogue as a sinister sound, the lilting note that preceded the smack in the face. Yet I felt strangely at home here. The barmaid was a dead-ringer for the guy who sat next to me in math. Another pint of Guinness and the band looked familiar. The whole country seems a vast high school reunion until you realize how little you have in common beyond a shared history that diverged a long time ago. Which is the ultimate discovery of any reunion. What I felt was the boozy glow of the alumnus who finally gives up looking for someone he knows and is happy just to be there. On this particular night, it seemed enough that we were all here, those who'd left and those who'd stayed. Together again.

Mornings I'd thaw out beneath the electric heater in the bathroom. Then I'd put on the kettle for tea and tune in the "Breakfast Show" on Radio Kerry. It was an odd mix of jokes, phone-in requests, and a running quiz for £100 of "fine Bavarian china." On the morning after St. Patrick's Day, the DJ filled a listener's eightieth birthday request with a scratchy recording of "I'll Take You Home Kathleen."

To where your heart will feel no pain
And where the fields are fresh and green.

My wife stopped drying her hair and listened transfixed. "My grandmother always sang that song. I used to think she was singing it to my older sister and it made me jealous."

The next selection, which came from a School of the Week in Ennis and sounded as if it had been recorded in a gymnasium, looked to the future rather than the past. A music teacher beat out the melody of "New York, New York" on a piano while a young girl sang the lyrics in a wavering, hopeful voice: *These little town blues are melting away.*

Dogs Playing Poker

Two hours of tunneling through darkness and I'm on the home-
stretch, a tense dozen miles through state forest that would be less
white-knuckled if not for the deer. Herds of them. They look innocent enough in daylight in their red summer coats, especially the
does with fawns, but at night, eyes ablaze in the ditches, they loom
like suicide bombers. My only collision occurred on another stretch
of road in broad daylight when the deer, bounding dog-like alongside the car, surprised both of us by abruptly changing course, a decision that cost me a radiator and the deer its life. Tonight, however, they remain on the periphery of my headlights. Then it's over
the river and through the woods and I'm at the cottage door fum-
bling for the keys and the breaker switch. When the lights come on,
so does the radio. I keep the dial tuned to WOJB, a public radio station on the Lac Courte Oreilles Indian Reservation, whose volun-
teer dee-jays host an eclectic mix of programs. Tonight, thank God,
is Honky Tonk Saturday and not the Pow-Wow Show or Global
Beat or what my wife calls the Dissonance Hour. Having driven one

hundred miles to be alone, what I want most at the moment is to hear another voice, even if it's the mournful, hillbilly voice of Kitty Wells singing "How Far Is Heaven?" When I arrive this way, late and alone, there's a lingering sense of being in-transit, suspended between home and away-from home. Even the cottage decor—old board games, a deer skull, a framed print by C. M. Coolidge, crossed snowshoes, a family photograph when the children were young—suggests people who haven't made up their minds.

After a beer or three, I'll step outside. The outhouse was torn down last summer, but I usually forego indoor plumbing on first arrival for a balancing act on the edge of the deck. The dark, so absolute from inside, materializes into an overgrown yard sloping to the river. Panels of window light fall upon the deck swirling with moths. Legs splayed, I keep my balance despite the river's sliding motion and the arc of my own small stream. If I look up too quickly, stars will blur into streaks and commas like a time-lapse photograph of the night sky in which the stationary focal point is me. It's all I can do to keep from falling off the earth.

The first sound in the morning is my neighbor's dump truck rumbling over the bridge. Roy Gilge is a timber cruiser for the state forest and does freelance excavating on weekends. Sometimes he'll stop by after work to talk about our common interests, fishing conditions or the stingy management of the dam upriver. Since we're about the same age and married later in life, we've both had the experience of raising small children while presiding over the deteriorating health of our parents, a vantage point from which one can see with equal clarity the past and the future. We have the only houses on this side of the river although Roy lives in his year round. It is his home, in other words, the seat of domestic life and responsibility, while mine is more of an escape from those things. When the Gilges want to escape, they drive to a cabin on a nearby lake.

Roy's father subdivided this land along the Elk River in the 1950s and sold the lots for $100 each. The red pine he planted to serve as boundaries now tower overhead. He also built a red, two-room cabin with the dimensions of a box car that stood on my lot until I tore it down. The original owner was a mystery man named Peg Leg Bill, who stiffed the well driller and ended up with a 42-foot well but no plumbing. The next owners, weekenders from Illinois, would drive six hours to drink beer and warm themselves with a bonfire pilfered from the Gilges' woodpile. The place had been on the market for three years when I bought it and built a new cottage. Roy's wife was cordial when we first met but allowed how hard it was seeing somebody else move in. "We've had the area to ourselves for so long." I like to think I was an improvement on the others though the best neighbor is undoubtedly no neighbor at all.

Originally, I'd built the cottage as a gathering place for extended family to renew their bonds over canoe trips and badminton—and every Fourth of July this is more or less the case. When I'm here alone, though, it seems more like a big box. Who as a child has not crawled into a cardboard box that once sheltered a major appliance and now shelters him? A Freudian might regard this holing up in boxes as a symbolic return to the womb, but it's just an early effort to make a private space for oneself. You crawl into the box on hands and knees and think: Nothing can touch me now. The balancing act is knowing when to crawl out. A colleague of mine built a cabin in the woods to which he increasingly retreated. One weekend he returned to find a note from his wife on the dining room table. She was leaving him. In the divorce settlement, however, he got the house then sold the cabin because he no longer needed an escape, or else, as I suspect, the place became too lonely with no home to back it up.

I love sitting on the deck in the morning watching the sun burn through the mist along the river. Here is the good life so familiar from outdoor clothing catalogues and advertisements for breakfast foods. You sit on the deck in your Adirondack chair drinking a really, really great cup of coffee.

What to do with the day? If I launched my canoe here and followed the circuitry of rivers downstream—Elk River to the South

Fork to the Flambeau to the Chippewa—the current would deliver me in a few days to a gravel bar opposite the office building where I work. Never mind the intervening waterfalls and hydroelectric dams and class IV rapids, who'd make such a long, pointless commute? There are plenty of chores here. I have been applying mortar and field stone to the block chimney at a rate that won't reach the roof for another year. There's a new woodshed to build and a tile hearth for the woodstove. I always bring my toolbox to the cottage and as I walk out the door my wife always asks, "Why can't you fix things here?" The answer is simple. One is work and the other play.

Lately I've been helping out a friend who is a tax assessor for some northern townships and, in the process, learning more about my fellow cottagers. Americans own 5.1 million vacation homes, ten percent of which were purchased last year alone. Sometimes they seem to have all taken up residence in northern Wisconsin although this cannot be true. The township we've been measuring includes pricey lake homes on the Turtle-Flambeau Flowage near the border with Upper Michigan. My friend has a magnetized ASSESSOR sign attached to the door panel so that people living at the end of a long, secluded driveway will know why we're there. Unless it's a weekend, few of the residents are home. If they are, they're not happy to see us. My 100-foot reel of measuring tape might as well be a flaming sword to drive them from paradise.

"My neighbor is building a new home," one man complained, his face livid. "He paid $250,000 for the lot. I paid $25,000. Why should I pay the same as these millionaires?"

He should be happy that his second home is increasing in value by double-digits instead of ratting on his neighbor. But I didn't tell him that. I told him that I was just measuring the outside dimensions of his buildings to draw a footprint of the property and had nothing to do with assigning values, which my friend would do later. Since the bulk of property taxes goes to the state, even a township with no school can be an expensive place to live.

Driving around a lake, one looks hard for what E. B. White once described as *cottages with their innocent and tranquil design, their tiny docks with the flagpole*. He was writing about cottages built around or before the Second World War, often of vertical logs painted mint green or bright yellow and set upon a fieldstone foundation, structures built with no intention of duplicating the house where the family lived the rest of the year. The new houses going up around the lakeshore measure in the thousands of feet with multiple decks and dormered roofs in a style that could hardly be called "innocent." These are not cottages in the traditional sense but investment strategies, a hedge against the stock market, over-built with an eye on resale.

"I've got a pie-shaped lot," one owner sighed. "There's no room for my toys."

We were standing at the end of a cul-de-sac with three new summer houses that would not look out of place in suburban Chicago. The owner of the middle house had an attached two-car garage but no pole buildings like his neighbors' in which to store boats and all-terrain vehicles and various equipment for the good life.

It was hard working up sympathy for him when just a stone's throw from the lake you're looking at Tobacco Road. I'd just come from measuring a one-story house down the road that was sheathed in pink asphalt siding. The front yard of packed dirt was guarded by a pair of growling mastiffs. I waited in the car until the owner appeared, an enormous man in overalls and no shirt. "The dogs is harmless," he said, and led them away. The house was bigger than its narrow front suggested, additions like shoe boxes laid end-to-end. Measuring the distances, I could see fragments of deer bone mixed in the dirt and weeds.

During the summer, rich and poor live in the kind of proximity one associates with Central American republics but with less animosity. Locals understand that summer people prop up an otherwise shaky economy, while the well-heeled cottager is apt to view the fellow in the trailer down the road as a less ambitious version of himself even though the local may be holding down two jobs just to keep his head above water. On the other hand, the summer resident may also suspect he's being chiseled by the local plumber or singled out unfairly for higher taxes because of the out-of-state license plate on his car. In fact, some locals keep their assessments low by letting the house go unpainted, while the cottager invests heavily in cedar shakes and expensive window groupings precisely to make a showy presentation to relatives and guests: *Welcome to the cabin.*

Middle-class families who couldn't dream of affording a summer home used to be able to rent one by the week or impose on relatives, which is what my family did. The places were invariably small cabins clustered around a central dock. They came furnished with thrift-shop curtains and lumpy beds, the use of a small boat, and often a library of swollen paperbacks, usually Westerns, which, if you took one home to finish, retained the slightly rancid smell of the cabin. Some resort owners bolstered their income by running a bar where families could escape a rainy afternoon, the children playing pinball while their parents drank beer. Such mom-and-pop resorts are becoming scarcer, however, as owners find it more profitable to sell the property outright than renting it piecemeal over many summers. I measured the remains of just such a place on Boot Lake, a tavern-resort that occupied its own skinny peninsula along with a handful of tumble-down cabins. The place had recently been sold to an out-of-state doctor, who, at great expense, propped up the tavern so he could replace its original foundation with poured cement walls. It would have been cheaper to demolish the building and start fresh, but this way kept the new owner on the lake without having to meet the state's current setback of sixty-five feet for new construction.

On the other side of the lake, the shoreline was steeper and the houses correspondingly more modest. At the end of the road, an older woman came out leaning heavily on her cane and sat down to visit at a picnic table surrounded by ceramic bears and plaster gnomes. Years ago she would drive up from Illinois with her children to stay at the resort across the lake. The resort owner apparently spent a lot of time patronizing his own tavern but offered clean and affordable cabins.

"It was a family place, you know? A place people could take their children."

Summers at the lake had been such happy times for the woman that she'd bought this property and moved up after retiring with the idea of extending those brief, sunny weeks into years. Then her daughter moved to California, and her son, who lived nearby, died suddenly of throat cancer, and she found herself terribly alone. At this point in the story she was sobbing and complaining how the neighbors kept their distance though she was so starved for company that it was easy to see why. She'd retired to the north woods for solitude, for the "peace and quiet" as she put it, and now it had arrived like a life sentence.

Sometimes I'd leave the car at a gated driveway to walk a mile or more into the woods, never quite knowing what to expect—a secluded hunting camp or a meth lab. My assessor friend once found bear traps hidden in the tall grass beside some out-buildings at the end of one of these secluded roads. They hadn't been set, but the message was clear enough. Following a dirt track through the forest, I once came upon a gingerbread house of timber and stucco, a rather grand place with its own private lake and stick-built gazebo. Nobody appeared to have been there for at least a year as a note from the previous assessor was still stuck in the screen door. Measuring the front porch, I peered through a dusty window to see a wooden carousel horse ridden by a toy monkey. A somber moose head looked down from the wall. When I leaned closer to look through another window, I heard a high-pitched screeching from the eaves and saw a mound of bat guano beneath the window sill. The place gave me the creeps.

Deserted houses always beg the question of why the people left, and while drug busts could account for some quick departures, most of these places had an air of domestic tragedy. One time, measuring with my wife, we came upon the shell of a new house that appeared to have been abandoned in mid-construction. There were new brass light fixtures flanking the massive front door but elsewhere the house was unfinished, sheets of plywood weathered to a dull silver.

"What do you think?" I asked my wife. "He run out of money?"

"I'd say he ran out of marriage."

Two alternating currents exert a constant pull on our lives. One is to stay put and the other is to hit the road. A second home is an attempt to have it both ways, a home you travel to, a place both distant and familiar. For a long time, my wife and I found one home enough to manage, and when the travel bug hit we would load the kids in the car and go camping. As our family grew, so did the size of the tent. We went through a two-man tent, then a four-man dome, until I finally bought a tent large enough to stand up inside, a six-man affair with a formidable name, something like "The Commander" or "The Headquarters" or "The Last Redoubt." But it was still a tent, which meant sleeping on the ground and putting up with noisy drunkards at state parks and smelling like a wet campfire when the rains came. We started looking for property up north.

At a certain season in our life we are accustomed to consider every spot as the possible site for a house. I suspect that the season Thoreau was referring to was his own age at the time of Walden, his twenties, when the choice of where to live implies as well a choice of how to live. Buying a second home in middle age is not the same as going into the woods in one's twenties because what's risked is disposable income rather than one's future. It's life in the country without having to make a living in the country. In my mid-twenties I built a cabin in Alaska, intending to live in the woods though lacking the basic skills to do so. Even the most domestic of chores, like cooking, took on an elemental aspect when done over a propane stove by lantern light. For the first time, I felt as if I was living *deliberately*. Leaving at the end of that summer, I maintained the fiction of returning on a permanent basis. But subsequent stays never lasted more than a week, and I kept my day job. This was not a home, in other words, but a vacation home; somehow I'd put the cart before the horse. On the other hand, when my sister dropped out of college to live on a hilltop in northern Washington state years ago, she forfeited other options. She and her husband picked apples and raised goats as well as children in a Little House version of life that may have grown old before the kids did. They stuck it out until the kids were grown then moved to Seattle.

My guide in the search for a cottage was my best friend, the tax assessor. We'd met twenty years ago when he was eking out a living as a nonunion carpenter, and I had just moved to Wisconsin. After Alaska, the countryside seemed unrelentingly flat except for the rivers, which tumbled like white staircases through the woods. One afternoon some friends and I kayaked on Slough Gundy, three short pitches of rapids on the South Fork of the Flambeau before the river plummets over a ten-foot waterfall. I'd pulled my kayak ashore and was drying off on a rock when a friend galloped past shouting that some fool was going to run the falls in an open canoe. A granite island splits Little Falls into two distinct chutes. The right chute is impossibly stacked with boulders; the left chute is a sheer drop. I'd managed to climb onto the island where somebody handed me an 8mm movie camera and asked if I'd record the attempt. My recollections of that day are forever framed by the camera's viewfinder. I am below the falls, so the river to the right of it appears as a thin, watery horizon. Now the canoeist hoves into view, a large man kneeling just ahead of the center thwart. Backpaddling, he expertly keeps the canoe perpendicular to the falls. The bow extends over the lip of the falls until half the canoe is poised in midair. Then everything goes wrong. Slowly the canoe begins to pivot until it flips upside down and disappears into the pool of oxygenated water below. At this point, I stopped filming. After what seemed a very long count, a tennis shoe bobbed to the surface.

Then the blade of a broken paddle. At last the canoeist himself broached, a big fellow with a reddish-blonde beard. Turning slowly on his back, he kicked to shore. That's how I met Bob Elkins.

By the time he started helping me look for property, Bob had gone from carpentry work to real estate appraiser and then tax assessing. Each career move, he liked to point out, paid him more for doing less physical work. He also speculated in real estate in a modest way, sniffing out properties overlooked by full-time realtors— lots with house trailers or vacant forties or marshy lake lots ("soft frontage")—which he'd advertise in Milwaukee newspapers for city dwellers looking for their own piece of paradise: *Cozy farmhouse with orchard! Hunt out your back door!* Sometimes he'd talk himself into buying a place and fixing it up. Then when it began to seem like an albatross around his neck, he'd sell and take off on a motorcycle trip.

For two years we chased around the north woods, tracking down little hunting cabins or Rip Van Winkle farmsteads where the owners had simply slipped away and let the pasture grow up in aspen. One old farmhouse on the Jump River was wreathed in blackberry brambles and had a stone silo like a medieval tower. Wriggling through an open window, we found the place intact except for the dust and flies on the cracked linoleum floor. There were dishes in the kitchen and a farm implement calendar hanging on the wall that read 1965. What had once been somebody's farm, the home place, had become over the years a hunting camp, perhaps where the family reassembled each November, and then finally a ruin. Bob could not look at a tumble-down farmhouse or cabin without imagining fresh paint on the shutters or a row of newly planted apple trees, then converting the improvements into dollars and cents. Lacking imagination, all I could see was the wreck where somebody had dead-ended.

Whenever I got discouraged, Bob would send a letter describing another golden opportunity. *"I have been sucking coffee and elbowing some mutual friends for information on the seller. I need to get to the courthouse in Ladysmith and get to the bottom on liens and what type of deed is recorded. In this poker game, it's best to see where the other person is coming from."*

The property was a landlocked 160-acre farmstead that would or would not come on the market. Getting there required a bush-whacking canoe trip down the Thornapple River and over a dozen beaver dams until we emerged from an alder canopy into the wider valley. It was a brilliant Indian summer day and some of the ridge-top maples had already flamed a bright crimson. We beached the canoe below a clearing in the woods and climbed a grassy knoll that had once been a farmstead. Its owner, John Deitz, had been some-thing of a national celebrity around the turn of the last century, a Populist hero who'd held off logging barons and sheriff's posses with a Winchester. A photograph of Deitz's place taken in the win-ter of 1905 showed a barn, root cellar, and squat house, all built of log, on the open hillside among protruding stumps. Now nothing remained of the farm or Deitz's notoriety, no ruined buildings or commemorative marker, nothing but an overgrown hole in the ground where the root cellar once stood that was ringed with chalky wolf scat.

When John Deitz moved his family to the Thornapple in 1904, most of the white pine forests of northern Wisconsin had been re-duced to stumpage, and logging barons like Frederick Weyer-haeuser were selling off their holdings prior to moving operations to the Pacific Northwest. Land companies, aided by the state agri-cultural college, promoted what was called The Cutover as pro-ductive farmland. A flood of immigrants, mainly Scandinavians and Slavs, settled here only to find poorly drained soils and a growing season too brief for raising cash crops. (After forty years of forest-to-farm promotion, only six percent of northern Wis-consin was in cultivation, a figure that would be further eroded by the Great Depression as tax delinquencies actually reversed the process.) The son of a German emigrant, Deitz had massive hands, narrow blue eyes, and a stubborn streak. After patching together a living as a logger/farmer and hunting guide, he bought the Thornapple land from a widow for $1.75 an acre, a real bargain even if there was only a wagon trail to the nearest town. Then he struck a bigger bonanza when he realized that a logging dam owned by the Chippewa Lumber & Boom Company was actually located on a corner of his new property. The following spring when Weyerhaeuser's loggers came to open the sluice gates and send the last of the white pine logs down the Thornapple, Deitz drove them off at gunpoint. He demanded back-pay from the company as well as thousands of dollars for all the timber that had previously come through the dam. The stand-off lasted two years and involved shoot-outs and ambushes on both sides. The logging company hired a train-car load of private detectives in Chicago and sent them into the woods to lay siege to Deitz, but the farmstead's commanding position overlooking the valley gave him a tactical advantage. The public regarded Deitz as a hero for taking on the Lumber Trust, not a violent blackmailer. Sympathetic newspapers printed his rambling manifestos and occasional efforts at verse:

Hold the fort, for I am coming,
With my pepper gun;
Watch the smoke and watch the shooting—
Watch the sheriff run!

Weyerhaeuser finally ended the dispute with a cash settlement to get his logs moving, but Deitz's troubles with the law didn't end. A few years later, he drew his Luger in a fight in town, wounding a man in the neck. When a posse surrounded the log home on the Thornapple, Deitz shot and killed a deputy and went to prison, just another backwoods hothead.

Bob and I ate our lunch on a sunny knoll overlooking the river. Downstream we could see the remains of the old cobbled dam and the tall masts of a few white pine that had escaped the loggers towering now over the surrounding forest. The climax forest nostalgically known as the North Woods is long gone and the Cutover with it, succeeded by a mixed bag of third and fourth-growth forests. Popple, not pine, is what keeps timber companies afloat in northern Wisconsin, the forest continuously harvested for pulpwood to supply the nation with cardboard boxes and bum's wipe. Facing the long paddle upstream, I'd given up any thought of buying Deitz's farmstead. Still, it wasn't hard to imagine his persistent grip on the land. In every tavern, you hear the same carping by men who feel passed over, the same fantasies of holding off the bad guys at gunpoint although the bad guys these days are more likely to be cast from the government rather than corporations.

"In real estate, there is an ass for every saddle. Your ass fits this one, pal. With minor alterations (paint) the property should bring in the teens (no problem). VERY LOW PAYMENT. YOU CANNOT LOSE MONEY, IF YOU DECIDE YOU DON'T LIKE IT."

The saddle in question was a two-room cabin on the South Fork of the Flambeau half-buried in snow. I was still mulling over the possibilities on the drive home when I ran into the deer. A bad omen.

A few months later, Bob sent me a flyer for a cabin on the Elk River. His handwritten comments in the margins played tug-of-war with my real estate sensibilities. *"Lot is good but small. Rapids out the front door! Bad window placement. She needs some jerking. Mostly cosmetic."*

The accompanying photograph showed a long, narrow shack with a low roof and few windows. But I wasn't looking at the building. I was looking at the dark slice of river in the left background with white rents where boulders split the surface of the water. Rapids out the front door.

After a cursory inspection tour with my wife in which the recreational possibilities of the river were emphasized and the cabin's cramped quarters and pet-shop smell glossed over, we bought the place. I'd paid more than Bob recommended though less than the asking price since the property had been on the market three years, about the price of a used car. After a single, sleepless night listening to squirrels running relay races in the cabin roof, we decided to tear it down.

A certain coolness of nerve is required to take a Sawzall and crowbar to a structure you've just paid good money for, yet I could see that no amount of "jerking" was going to transform this cabin into a cottage. The distinction was clear in my mind. A cabin's walls are tacked with grouse fans and beer calendars; dresser drawers brim with cartridge boxes. There is an absence of furniture but plenty of floor space for friends to roll out sleeping bags on opening weekend. A cottage, on the other hand, is light and airy and less obviously selfish. Summer days the family would sun themselves on the deck and play Yahtzee or Kings-in the-Corner after dinner. In winter the children would sprawl before the woodstove reading *Wind in the Willows*, quietly repeating its quaint British locutions: "Bother" and "Oh Blow." I wanted Toad Hall on the river, and this sorry dump wasn't it.

The most beautiful house in the world, the architect Witold Rybczynski assures us, is the one we build ourselves. This presumes that we know what we're doing. I may have lacked carpentry skills but, luckily, had a friend who didn't. After Bob shot the site with a transit, we poured the cement slab then framed up the stud walls with sixteen-penny nails and a framing hammer. The dimensions were modest, 24 feet by 24 feet, the size of a two-car garage. When we sheathed it in Blandex, I foolishly thought: We're half-way done! Weeks soon turned into months. Into this box we fitted a kitchen, a bedroom, a tiny bathroom, a combination dining and living area, and a half-loft. We hung a dozen factory-second windows, so the place wouldn't seem like a garage. Friends were enlisted to screw down the steel roof, a tricky business requiring several ladders and no fear of heights. When the plumber hooked up Peg Leg Bill's old well to the new copper pipes and cold, clear water poured from the kitchen tap, it seemed a miracle.

Occasionally, however, I realized that some things had been lost in the process. I could no longer hear the river from inside or rain drumming on the roof. The bald eagle whose daily flight upstream had been a reward for working on the roof now flew overhead without an audience. And one weekend I returned to find the drywaller had left the windows and door open between sandings to air out the dust. When I switched off the lights that evening, lightning bugs transformed the loft into a planetarium show.

We look back fondly on the phase known as "building the cottage" in the same way that married couples look back nostalgically on courtship as that time when everything was possible. In my memory of this time, the weather is always fine, the fish are biting, and nobody would dare think of some place she'd rather be. But thumbing through my journal, I see that the weather notations are a mixed bag, the river occasionally rain-swollen and too high to fish. Our then-twelve-year-old daughter recorded her dissatisfaction: "Aug. 8—we better leave tonite. I'm board."

My first memory of a place not home was a lake cottage outside of Dowagiac in the sandy farmland of southwestern Michigan. It didn't belong to my family but to a distant cousin, a cigar-smoking priest from Chicago who drove like a madman and wore a black, collarless shirt. The lake wasn't wild but had a shallow, weedy end where each dusk a great blue heron stalked among the cattails looking for frogs. There was a on rib-and-plank canoe, which my older brother was allowed to take by himself. We would watch him paddle away from the dock and disappear into the reeds only to emerge an hour later with a mess of yellow perch and bullheads. In this way, we felt we were learning about the world. There was a rock grotto of the Blessed Virgin periodically overrun by hordes of small toads. There was a dank basement that smelled of canvas life preservers and housed a slot machine as well as a private chapel. A spinster aunt kept us supplied with ice cream cones which we secretly broke into wafers and served at pretend masses in the basement chapel while an older cousin mumbled what he thought sounded like Latin. It was this mixture of nature and domesticity that I found so appealing as a child, more than, say, a visit to a ho-

tel where the only amusements were the elevator and little bars of
soap wrapped in paper. What I remember best of all about the cottage was a collection of framed prints by the stairs that depicted a
card party of cigar-smoking dogs. The dogs looked earnest about the
game and yet grinned as if contemplating a private joke. I remember some of the titles: "A Friend in Need," "A Bold Bluff," "Pinched
with Four Aces." In this last print, a bulldog and Boston terrier have
been collared by dogs dressed as Keystone Kops and brandishing
billy clubs. A literalist, I'd decided that the card-playing dogs had
been caught doing something they normally didn't—like taking pretend communion. That's how the entire week at the cottage struck
me, a happy parody of real life, only better because the adults didn't
go to work and you never took off your bathing suit except to sleep.

In the past year three friends of mine departed this world so
suddenly, as if taken up in a space ship, that the rest of us began
wondering when our own numbers might be called. Reaching
fifty, some people accelerate the pace of their careers or else jump
ship for some new pursuit because of a sense of time running out.
Trips are made, expeditions mounted. The idea is to imprint as
many new sights and experiences on the mind as possible as if it
was a retirement account on which one could draw on the interest alone. Holing up in a cottage, on the other hand, represents an
opposite tack because the main attraction is constancy. It's the
long view over time. Every June a snapping turtle hauls herself up
from the river to lay her eggs in the warm sandy ground by the
bridge, and every summer a raccoon digs the eggs out and eats
them. Any cottage journal soon becomes a record of phenome-
nology—wildflowers that appear on schedule, birds coming or going. Even the sunlight runs on a tight loop. In May it's a polarizing
lens that makes the trees look greener and the sky bluer; by October it's lost considerable heat but, coming from beneath a gray
storm-front, can strike the rapids downstream like a searchlight.
When my children were little and still enthralled with nature, they
enjoyed the cottage on exactly these terms. They captured garter

snakes and crayfish with an enthusiasm that suggested the world was a one-time-only garage sale. Now that they're teenagers and caught up in their own social fish bowl, it's circularity that bores them: the idea that nature repeats itself so predictably. Prisoners of time, they don't want to miss the moment. When they do come up north, they're most attuned to people. They drive to the local movie theater and feel sophisticated because their peers back home don't neck unabashedly in the cineplex and the projectionist doesn't have to stop the film to change reels.

After Labor Day, most of the summer places go dark. Resorts close and the roads are deserted; it's as if some disaster had forced a general evacuation. Traffic won't pick up until late November when deer season begins. Every fall I watch the man who owns the land across the road drive an ATV into the woods with a sack of feed corn. He is baiting deer to improve his odds of shooting a big buck on opening day. Of course, my real fear is that the rumors are true and he plans to sell the eighty acres upriver to a developer, at which point I'll feel like Roy Gilge did when I moved in. He works in a cardboard factory in the nearest town and inherited the land, so it represents a windfall for him—a different kind of escape.

Hunting in northern Wisconsin is more difficult than in the agricultural south because there are expansive forests, not just woodlots, and the deer have more places to hide. But I don't bait because it seems to side-step a vital aspect of hunting, namely the hunting. As a result, I haven't shot a deer in three years. Nevertheless, I've covered a lot of territory, mostly newly logged openings in the county forest or large blocks of the Kimberly Clark Wildlife Area the state burns every few years for sharp-tail grouse habitat. Once when I told a DNR wildlife biologist where I hunted, he showed me a photograph of six pairs of tracks wolves left in the snow as they trotted shoulder-to-shoulder like teenagers down the same road I walk each November. Hiking a snow-covered road is one way to take a wildlife census of the area, and lately I've found fewer tracks of porcupine and more fisher, fewer grouse but more trident tracks of wild turkey. It's nice to consider that we're not the only creatures extending our range though we're certainly the keystone species, the ones the others have most to fear. Last opening morning of deer season I was lingering over coffee when I looked out the cottage window to see a large buck in my yard. It was undoubtedly the same old buck that the landowner across the road had baited all summer. I sat at the table watching the buck hesitate in the predawn gloom as a pair of headlights approached; then he bounded over the bridge and into the woods, safe at least for another day.

The Deer in the Tree

In northern Wisconsin the change of seasons can be abrupt enough to feel like a border crossing. Autumn in particular brings to mind a small republic that we cross too quickly on the way to winter, leaving behind a certain language not to mention cuisine. You rush to put up storm windows and quarts of vegetables, collect windfalls from the orchard, drive around to see peak colors before rainstorms beat them from the trees, trying urgently to gather everything that ripens before it's gone because autumn is both harvest time and the season of loss.

The garden is the first to go. All summer I've followed its progressions, through salad days to the rigors of canning tomatoes when the kitchen steams like a Turkish bath and the sink overflows with Burpee Big Boys and Beefsteaks my wife is putting up against the certainty of winter. Then one morning you awake to a chill in the air, and while the maple blazing in the front yard is in its finest hour, the tomato vines are terminal cases. After the first hard frost has leveled the garden, we pick through the wreckage to salvage, among the acorn squash and onions, a few hard, green tomatoes to set on the windowsill in hopes of ripening.

My kitchen window looks out on a Norway spruce that casts the only shade in the backyard since the elms died. Last year I sawed off the lower limbs and hung a bird feeder to attract goldfinches and the odd grosbeak. Then, a few days before Thanksgiving, a friend helped me hang a whitetail deer from the same branch. It was an awkward business. I stood on a step ladder, hauling on the rope while my friend propped the deer up from underneath. When he let go, the branch sagged under the dead weight, but my slip-knot held and the deer's hooves stopped dangling a foot or so above the bed of spruce needles.

As long as the temperature hovered above freezing, I intended to hang the carcass before butchering so enzymes in the meat would tenderize it. There wasn't room in the garage to hang the deer where, strung up in the dark among bicycles and garden rakes, it would have only seemed more tragic. Outside in the cold sunlight, its long neck stretched beneath a canopy of spruce boughs, the deer looked appalling enough.

My friend, who lives out-of-state, said, "If I did this in my back-yard, the neighbors would string *me* up!"

But where I live, northern Wisconsin, the opening of deer hunting season remains a secular day of obligation. Factories close and schools run half-empty. Parties of armed men sweep across harvest fields and woodlots, gunfire punctuating the crisp air, as if the whole countryside had been given over to an elaborate Civil War reenactment. The local TV station sponsors a Big Buck contest, and in every Main Street cafe the waitress asks, by way of greeting, "Get your deer yet?" There's raunchy entertainment in the taverns for the hunters and, on alternate nights, a Deer Widows Ball featuring male strippers for their lonesome wives. It gets strange.

Nobody equates killing deer with gardening, but it's not euphemistic to speak of both as a harvest if one hunts for meat and

not horns. I don't believe, as Joseph Wood Krutch wrote, that hunting as sport is "pure evil." We have animals slaughtered every day
for which we feel no guilt. Raising a calf to slaughter does not seem
the kind of cruelty that killing a deer does because we don't identify with livestock in ways we do with wildlife. Nobody speeds past
a slow-moving stock truck on the way to the next burger joint and
asks: Where are they going? Where have they come from? Gradu-
ally you begin to suspect an absence of narrative in this Happy
Meal existence. Hunting becomes, if it is to have any value, a story
connecting the life of the game with your own.

Opening morning had found me standing in the predawn gloom of
a boat landing, helping a friend wrestle a canoe into the Chippewa
River. Paddling upstream in the dark, I dropped my flashlight into
the water where it continued to send a greenish beam slanting up
from the river bottom even after we hauled the canoe ashore.
Scouting before season, I'd picked a stand on a narrow isthmus of
dry land overlooking an active game trail and managed to find it in
the dark. At first light, there was an opening barrage of gunfire to
the south, then nothing but the distant rumble of freight cars over
the Burlington Northern trestle. By noon, a cold drizzle changed
over into flurries. I busied myself watching the painstaking
progress of a nuthatch up the side of a burr oak and wondered what
I was missing back home.
    The Chippewa River bottoms lie in the transition zone between
the northern pineries and the open prairie to the west—prime deer
habitat. Walking these second-growth woods, it's hard not to imagine the people who hunted them before you and measure their mo-
tives against your own. In the early 1800s, the Ojibwe pushed the
Santee Sioux out of this territory because of its abundant game.
Coming upon fresh deer tracks, an Ojibwe hunter might sit down
and smoke a pipe filled with powdered aster root, the smoke of
which smells like a deer's hooves, and sooner or later a deer would
trot along the trail, sniffing the air. Like other hunting peoples, the

Ojibwe understood the paradox of killing in order to live. They treated the game with ritual and respect and thought it bad luck to brag about one's success in hunting, gestures most of us have long outgrown.

Across the Chippewa River in Pepin County is a replica of the cabin Charles Ingalls built his family in the 1860's, site of the "Big Woods" so vividly described by his daughter, Laura Ingalls Wilder. "Wolves lived in the Big Woods," she wrote, "and bears and huge wild cats." When her father returned from a hunt, he would hang the deer in a tree to keep it from the wolves. When my children were young, I took them to see the facsimile cabin on a bare hill next to the highway. Standing on that windy hilltop, I tried hard to imagine the Big Woods as it had been before being minced into pasturage and cornfields. There are still deer, more than during Laura's tenure or even the Ojibwes', but we're the only predators now. The others—wolves, bears, and panther—have either moved further north or disappeared from the state altogether, and they're not likely to come back.

At the end of the day, as I made my way along a narrow slough, I saw a movement about a hundred yards away. In hunting, the trick is to look for one feature, then build the animal around it. The first detail to give itself away was one dark eye, followed by a pair of semaphore ears and, lastly, the buff-colored deer itself. Four of them were moving single-file, sidling silently through the woods with a tip-toe gait. When I raised my gun, they broke from the trees, bounding down the slough, flags up. But there was no point in shooting as they made a furious beeline down the shore. Then, inexplicably, the deer decided to cross the slough on a narrow beaver dam. By the time I closed some of the distance, half the group had made it across. I aimed at the last deer—the largest— just starting to cross the dam and fired. At the sound of the shot, the deer suddenly hesitated, perking up her ears, then sagged to the ground even as the others disappeared into the oak woods.

When I got to the beaver dam, I didn't see the deer at first and worried that I'd botched the shot. Then I saw the carcass motionless in the tall grass beside the dam, eyes already skinned over in the cold.

Later, I rendezvoused with a friend who'd shot a large buck and was dragging it back to the canoe. Even taking turns doubleteaming on the drag-lines, we didn't reach the river until dusk. Then we drifted downstream, deer between the thwarts, slush ice rubbing against the sides of the canoe. There was the sense, as the river froze, of autumn closing irretrievably behind us. It was dark when we pulled up at Fox Coulee Landing. A crowd stood around to gawk as deer were swung out of boats by their fetlocks and tied onto car roofs in a half-circle of headlights.

Bushey's Bar in Urne was jammed with orange hats, so we sat on barstools waiting for a table. Thirteen deer racks were arranged on the pine walls in progressively larger sizes so as to suggest evolution. Before rural consolidation, the barroom had been the township school and the adjoining Quonset-roofed dining room its gymnasium. A pool player with deltoid sideburns announced loudly, "I went to second grade right here!" When a table opened, we took our drinks into the old gym and ordered the chicken buffet. The waitress pulled a pencil from her hairdo. "Well boys," she said without enthusiasm, "get your deer yet?"

It's easier to explain hunting in terms of meat rather than sport. "Sport" implies gamesmanship and trophy mongering—killing as fun. Even critics of hunting qualify their opposition with a grandfather clause for subsistence hunters. But few people hunt today out of sheer necessity; it's almost always a choice, in other words, a sport. The only time I ever hunted out of anything like necessity was in Alaska when I was out of work. Hunting the spruce hills behind my cabin, I missed my only shot at a bull moose. Back in Fairbanks, I applied for food stamps, which a friend sneeringly referred to as my "paper moose," meaning I had gotten the meat without bloodying my hands. Even now, paying cash at the supermarket like everyone else, I still think of the "paper moose."

When he turned thirteen, my son thought he wanted to try hunting, so I enrolled him in a hunter's education class at the rod and gun club. Three nights a week I'd pick him up after football practice and we'd drive out of town in the waning October light. The rod and gun club sat in the middle of a pine plantation through which shooting lanes had been cut for skeet and target practice. Inside, the club-house had a horseshoe-shaped bar (closed during instruction) where I sat with other parents. The knotty-pine walls were hung with smoke-tinted deer heads and a Norman Rockwell–style print above the fireplace. Entitled "Carrying on the Tradition," the picture showed an old geezer holding forth on a front porch with a carbine in his hands while an improbable group of clean-cut, racially diverse teenagers listened in rapt attention—quite unlike the squirming, winking bunch we'd brought.

The class offered some practical information, such as that you *aim* a rifle but *point* a shotgun, but most of the course revolved around handling firearms as opposed to the more esoteric notion of hunting. The instructors wore blaze orange vests and addressed the youngsters with the solemn portentousness of men telling ghost stories around a campfire. The chief lesson was to avoid shooting yourself or others. We watched video dramatizations of hunters killing or maiming each other as they fell dramatically off logs, tripped over fence wires, and blasted aimlessly at sounds in the woods. My son's lips moved as he silently read the title of yet another alarming hand-out, "I Shot My Best Friend."

I'd hoped the instructors would attempt to explain that hunting was more than firearms or trophies but was primarily a way of looking at country. You could cover miles and miles on foot and never fire a shot, yet you were *hunting* in the strictest sense of the word. You were looking for something with no guarantee of finding it

among the random clutter of the day. And even if you returned
empty-handed, you almost always brought back the story of what
you'd seen: a fox chasing a squirrel so intently that both nearly
jumped in your lap, a rat-tailed possum's slow progress across the
forest floor while you sat freezing in a tree, or the tattoo of tracks in
the snow that were themselves a story waiting to be interpreted.

But no such luck in the clubhouse. The lead instructor, an older
man with a permanent scowl, announced the first night that he ran
a "tight ship" and would brook no gum chewing, no smoking, and
no hats. Hearing this, some of the fathers at the bar removed their
hats. He used the scowl to menace the kids into silence, and the
message he imparted was that hunting is a brutal business, and it's
never too early to learn to be a bully. I never saw him smile except
once and that was when the class had moved outdoors to a shooting range. The night was clear and cold, the grass beneath the arc
lights quivering in its electric glow. As the instructor led the class
to the range, his breath came in quick puffs of smoke. He had a
joker's grin, really a smirk, on his face as if he couldn't wait to get
to the punch line. In one hand, he carried a .410 shotgun and in the
other a plastic milk jug filled with water. When he held the jug next
to some thatch-haired boy's head by way of comparison, I could see
what was coming. He placed the milk jug on the grass, slowly
backed up a few steps, then leveled the .410 and blew the jug to
smithereens.

One morning in 1960-something, I bicycled out to a fellow Boy
Scout's house in the countryside outside suburban Detroit. At scout
meetings, this boy's father looked like all the other fathers, a tired-
looking man who'd come directly from one of the Big Three au-
tomakers in a white shirt with the sleeves rolled up and tie undone.
But this morning he answered the door wearing a leather jerkin
and a quiver of arrows. He was going to give us archery lessons in
his extensive backyard, and the reward for those diligent boys who
showed up every week would be a deer hunting trip up north. The
only deer I'd seen were those my mother pointed out in power-line

cuts during the after-dinner drives we took when we rented a summer cottage. "There's a whole family!" she'd whisper as the car idled. The idea of potting one seemed ridiculous, like shooting a giraffe at the zoo. But I wanted to handle a recurve bow, which I'd seen used to such great effect in the movies. We spent a long, hazy morning shooting targets tacked to hay bales, which I imagined not as deer but as Prince John's evil henchmen, the arrows spurting up dust when they fell short. I quit the program long before the promised hunting trip to take up something else I'd seen in the movies—smoking—and the boys who did go up north returned complaining of a cold, uneventful weekend in the rain. At that age, hunting didn't seem brutal to me; it seemed pointless.

I came to hunting much later when I moved to Alaska in my twenties and met people for whom hunting seemed, if not necessary, at least relevant to their everyday lives. My instruction came at the hands of companions who showed an intensity for looking at country and a belief that the hunt neither began nor ended with a gunshot.

One fall, I joined a party of Hmong hunters, newcomers to the Midwest, to see if they hunted the same tangled river bottom any differently than I did. There were rumors that the Hmong could whistle like a fawn to attract does and possessed other sly tricks that put them at an advantage in the woods. We crossed a slough on a fallen log in the moonlight, then headed single-file through the tall grass, a column of small men carrying their rifles by the barrel, the stock slung over their shoulders. The adults in the party had grown up in the montane forests of northern Laos and had arrived in this country as refugees, having served it as surrogates in a secret war. Like so many midwesterners, they were displaced farmers who hunted as a link to the past as well as to reconnoiter new surroundings. Deer season represented a chance to revisit the people they had once been.

The only whistling I heard that day was by members of our party who whistled to communicate their location to each other. Joe Bee

Xiong, the party's leader, put me on a good stand overlooking a swale where he himself had planned to hunt. Sure enough, just after sunrise, I heard a shuffling of dry leaves as a young buck ran through the woods and down the trail toward me. It must have caught my scent as it drew abreast, pausing just before I fired as if remembering something important.

After the buck was down, I began the slow, reductive process of turning what was once alive into meat. Turning the deer over, I made a long incision with my sheath knife through the white belly hair and into the stretched drum of the diaphragm. All of it—the vaulted rib cage, the mammalian anatomy, the yeasty smell of blood and offal—seemed oddly familiar. Reaching up, I severed the windpipe so I could tip the entire paunch out onto the grass. I was separating the heart and liver from the pile when Joe Bee returned. He looked down at the steaming mess then retrieved the stomach, which he emptied by turning inside out like a purse, and cleaned it with snow. He said it tasted very good in stews.

We took three deer that day, including the buck, and brought them back to Joe Bee's duplex. A makeshift trestle table was erected in the backyard and lit with floor lamps brought from the house. In very short order the deer were skinned and butchered into ever smaller pieces until the table sagged. Then Joe Bee, as leader of the hunt, divided all of it—meat, bones, organs—into identical piles on a ground cloth. Twelve piles, one for each hunter. Sharing was the only difference I could see between Hmong hunting traditions and our own winner-take-all approach.

"If there had been only one deer and twenty hunters, " Joe Bee's brother told me, "there would be twenty piles."

That is what I wish my son had learned in hunter's education.

In 1929 when Aldo Leopold conducted a wildlife survey of north central states, he concluded that whitetail deer had been wiped out of southern Wisconsin except in isolated pockets along the Wisconsin River bottoms. The culprit was not so much hunting, which could be managed through bag limits and seasons, but habitat loss due to intensive agriculture. Leopold could be as rhapsodic as any naturalist in his elegies for disappearing species, but he was also a pragmatist who believed human intervention could occasionally restore what had been lost. This is the central thesis of Leopold's classic *Game Management:* "that game can be restored by the 'creative use' of the same tools which have heretofore destroyed it—axe, plow, cow, fire, and gun." Leopold was instrumental in moving wildlife management away from game wardens and into the hands of biologists who could be expected to take the longer view. When biologists speak of wildlife in terms of *range* or *carrying capacity,* they are using his words. It was Leopold's unwillingness to rule out the gun that keeps him the most controversial of the environmental prophets and the most relevant.

Time has borne out Leopold's theories, though in some cases to a degree unthinkable in his day. Southern Wisconsin now has one of the highest whitetail populations in the country, as many as 124 deer per square mile—so many that they threaten the regeneration of red and white oaks, the cornerstone of the oak savannah ecosystem. What Leopold could not have imagined is the change in landscape itself.

As marginal farms got converted to recreational tracts, the deer population exploded. The decline of small-scale agriculture coincided with a fundamental change in hunting practices. The traditions of farming are communal, which translated during hunting season into gang drives, a ragged line of men and boys strung across a forty-acre woodlot, pushing deer to designated shooters with terrible efficiency. Most farmers hunted for the table rather than horns, but if one took a trophy it was usually a buck the farmer had scouted from his tractor seat all summer. Hung on the dining room wall, the antlered head might gaze down upon the family meal like a kibitzer but not exactly as a stranger.

Today's landowner is more likely to see hunting as a competition rather than a cooperative venture. He posts the land to keep his neighbors from driving it though he might hire one to plant a few rows of feed corn. He invests in mineral blocks to boost antler growth and hangs motion-sensor cameras in the woods to locate potential trophy bucks that can "score" him into the Boone & Crockett record book. Because a single buck can inseminate a harem of does, the landowner who takes only trophy bucks has almost no effect upon the resident deer population except allow it to grow larger. This is our native genius for taking what is elemental and turning it into a contest.

In Buffalo County, a crosshatch of oak ridges and palmated valleys, this transformation was helped along by a local hunting guide who videotaped trophy bucks on scouting trips and edited an hour's worth into a popular hunting video called "Monster Valley." The video not only generated business for his guiding service but precipitated a steep rise in real estate values as the county's reputation for trophy whitetails grew nationwide. Two sequels followed: "Legend Lane" and "Monster Alley." In their episodic plot structure and breathless attention to secondary sex characteristics, they resemble pornographic movies. Horn Porn. They follow a predictable narrative. In the opening scene, a big buck, nicknamed "Garth" or "Elvis," is shown upright, caught by jacklight feeding in a cornfield. In the final scene, poor "Garth" lays supine on the forest floor, antlered head cradled tenderly in a hunter's arms as if the big buck had fallen asleep during the preliminaries and was now being roused to face the camera.

Hunting season is such a strange end to autumn. Sandwiched between Halloween and Thanksgiving, it manages to combine elements of both. There are the blaze-orange get-ups and weird personifications ("When the buck's away, shop our Lonely Doe Sale"), flashlights flickering in the dark, and the posturing of men with guns. On the other hand, there is also the companionship of friends and the anticipation of a feast, as well as the whiff of mortality that comes from knowing the true price of that feast.

For many years, an animal rights group in Madison marked the opening of deer season by strapping department store dummies dressed in blaze orange to their car fenders and driving in honking procession around the state capitol. Who could blame them? The annual parade was retaliation to the steady stream of deer carcasses, gutted and stiff, borne down state highways on car racks and tailgates. The message of the mock cortege was simple: Put yourself in the deer's place.

One year I joined an anti-hunting protest on opening day, not as a spy but as a self-assigned journalist. I wanted to see things from the other side. We'd assembled early that morning in the parking lot of a Hardee's off Madison's beltline and waited for a TV news crew to arrive—media being a necessary ingredient to any protest. There were coffee and rolls and good-natured joking although some of the younger protesters were understandably nervous. They'd been warned to wear blaze orange so hunters wouldn't blow their heads off. A nearby state park had been chosen because it was limited to hunters equipped with one-shot muzzle-loaders, who seemed somehow less murderous. Nobody wanted to look like Elmer Fudd, so many protesters showed up in bright plastic rain ponchos or crossing guard vests. I wore my old hunting jacket and hoped nobody would notice the bloodstained sleeves. When the film crew arrived, we caravaned down the interstate to Blue Mound State Park, tunneling through a pre-dawn forest, until the road opened to a clearing at the top. It was a cold night, the sky tracked with stars. We waited in the parking lot until a solitary car drove up. When the driver, an older man, stepped out and retrieved a muzzle-loader from the trunk, we swarmed him with ethical questions. Did he understand that killing animals was wrong? Did he value life over death? Had he ever considered hunting with a camera?

Caught like a deer in the glare of TV lights, the hunter shoved a cameraman, who shoved back. The floodlights rippled through the woods, casting immense shadows that made the struggle appear to be some strange campfire ceremonial. In the scuffle, the hunter dropped his car keys. "Look what you made me do!" he cried in a thin, pathetic voice. Embarrassed, we dropped to our knees to help him look. Finally, he found the keys, put the rifle back in the trunk, and drove away in the dark.

"That's one deer saved!" a fat woman in a traffic vest shouted. We all cheered.

Flushed with success, we fanned through the woods to look for other hunters. It was almost legal shooting time. Darkness ebbed as the forest solidified into separate trees, distinct in the gray, monochromatic half-light. It was like watching a photograph develop: oak trees and prickly ash and sloping ground covered with leaves. The sun was nearly up. Ahead on the trail, I could see the woman in the traffic vest. She was moving with quiet deliberation, placing her feet carefully so as not to make unnecessary noise; she had given herself wholly over to her senses—to what she could hear and see; she was living in time present, alert now to the landscape as it unfolded randomly around her. She was hunting.

Wolf at the Door

Flying high over the east fork of the Moose River, Richard Thiel listened for wolves. He sat behind the pilot, a map of northwestern Wisconsin spread across his knees, and followed the contours of the land. From 3,000 feet the woods below, with their snow-covered fire lanes and frozen creeks, looked like scrimshaw. On a clear day Thiel can pick up the *beep-beep* of any radio-collared wolf within a sixteen-mile radius. But this morning, in February 1981, the sky hummed with static.

Late in the previous spring, when these woods were hot and buggy, Thiel had trapped five wolves in this country, then the southernmost timber wolf territory in the United States. Before releasing the wolves, he fitted each with a lithium-powered radio collar. The collar transmits a signal that Thiel can pick up by means of antennae mounted on an airplane's wing struts. Now in winter, when wolves are most footloose, he was monitoring their range— eavesdropping from the sky in the morning and tracking on foot in the afternoon.

Flying north toward Solon Springs, Thiel picked up a faint pulse. He shouted over the engine's roar for the pilot to turn left and reduce altitude. The plane dipped down, converging on the transmitter until the signal was popping and the treetops were all a blur. Four whitetail deer were bedded down in a snowy clearing. At first glance Thiel mistook them for wolves. Then he spotted the pack, not two hundred yards away. Loping through the snow, the wolves seemed oblivious of the deer and even the shadow of the plane passing overhead.

The Eastern timber wolf, or gray wolf *(Canis lupus lycaon)*, once ranged over most of the eastern United States, from Maine to as far south as Georgia. According to mammalogist Hartley Jackson, as many as 20,000 wolves may have roamed in what is now Wisconsin when it was a forest known to the pioneers as the Big Woods. That figure seems exaggerated, though probably it wouldn't have to the earliest settlers. Diaries tell of granddad beating wolves from his horse-drawn cutter with a buggy whip and of hysteria rushed along by the howling of wolves—literally at the cabin door.

When the Big Woods were finally cut down, the surviving wolves melted into the roadless northern counties. Then the Great Depression put many men out of city jobs and into the woods. Work crews cut roads into forests, opening them up to trappers and hardscrabble farmers who could make a $20 bounty on a wolf, half that for a pup. The few surviving wolves became celebrated oddities.

Finally, sentiment began to build to keep a few wolves in northern Wisconsin, and in 1957 the state lifted the bounty. But it was too late. The wolves had gone the way of the Big Woods.

Growing up in suburban Milwaukee, Richard Thiel was a century too late to hear the wolf at the door. He knew the animal as most of us do: the ancestral dog that has not come to leash. Pity has replaced fear where our large predators are concerned. Ask Thiel why he studies wolves and he's likely to say he feels sorry for them. Trapped, shot, and poisoned on their former range, timber wolves had hung on in Minnesota and on Michigan's Isle Royale. But rumors persisted of an occasional wolf in northern Wisconsin—an uncertain glimpse, a few tracks on a sandy road.

Thiel began searching for these phantom wolves in the early '70s, spending summers and college weekends prowling the northern counties for wolf sign. He typed painstaking reports of his findings and sent them along, unsolicited, to the state's Department of Natural Resources. In August of 1974 Thiel and a fellow biology student at the University of Wisconsin–Stevens Point broadcast recorded wolf howls in the woods—using a tape player with the volume turned all the way up—to see if they could get a real wolf to howl back. One evening they were broadcasting from a canoe just after sunset, and they were about to quit for the night when a single timber wolf actually howled back. Thiel was so excited he forgot to start the tape on which they had hoped to get a recording of a howl. But he had some evidence! The next year, the state reclassified the wolf from extirpated to merely endangered.

Wisconsin's new wolves are almost certainly emigrants from neighboring Minnesota. Shut out by a sexually autocratic pack structure wherein only the dominant (alpha) pair breeds, the supposition goes, these loners headed southeast. They are the nucleus of Wisconsin's fragile wolf population. Thiel estimates there are fewer than thirty wolves in the state, but he believes Wisconsin could easily support as many as a hundred in heavily wooded areas where they could stay out of trouble.

Now head of the DNR's wolf study, Thiel functions as something of a front man for the wolves. He travels the high school and wildlife-club circuit, showing slides and assuring his audience that wolves are "wonderful critters." Thiel, 6′ 2″, with a reddish beard and a raptor's eyes, gives the impression of having just mushed into town. He shows slides of wolves and wolf scats. He calls himself a "scat man." The audience howls.

After one such presentation, I talked wolves with Thiel and hinted broadly that I'd like to go along the next time he cruised the woods.

"Wait till we get some tracking snow," he said.

Skidding down an unplowed forest road in Douglas County later that month, I kept my eyes peeled for wolf tracks. The three of us, Thiel, the driver, a soft-spoken DNR man named Larry Prenn, and I, were sandwiched into a ¾-ton pick-up. The snow was heavy and wet, good for tracking.

Earlier that morning Thiel had flown over a pack to the east; it was a tight group of seven wolves. Now we were driving the southern boundary of a pack with which Thiel had lost radio contact. Badly fragmented, this pack was down to a few wolves that seldom hung together. Thiel's only link to the group, a two-year-old male with ear-tag number 1187 and a radio collar, had been shot the week before. So now he had to track the remaining pack members on the ground.

Four white-tailed deer, walking in that tentative gait suggesting high-heel shoes, ambled down the middle of the road about a quarter of a mile from the truck. Halfway to them, Prenn braked. "Wolf tracks," he said.

One set of tracks, left by a wolf going at a slow trot, led from a frozen swamp onto a fire lane. Thiel measured the track, four broad toes and claw points, which seemed indistinguishable to me from that of a large dog. But it was, Thiel said, definitely wolf, and judging from the frost in the toe depressions, it had been made the day before. Following the tracks down the road, we were rewarded with a wolf scat.

Wolves have a scent gland that allows their scats, like their urination, to serve as scent posts to mark their territory. Scat analysis can show what wolves are eating and whether times are good or lean. Thiel suspects the wolves round out a diet heavy in deer with snowshoe hare in the winter and beaver in the summer.

Prenn broke off a twig and pushed the scat into a paper bag marked with the date and location. The bag went into the back of the pickup, joining at least fifty others. In the event of a sudden thaw, the truck was going to define a large territory of its own.

Since this scat was fairly fresh, Thiel decided to backtrack to see
what the wolf had been up to. Lunging into some alder brush, we
followed the tracks through knee-deep snow. Thiel took the lead.
We kept close behind, stepping into his footprints so we wouldn't
have to break our own trail. Wolves do the same thing to conserve
energy. A seemingly lone set of tracks through deep snow may have
accommodated an entire pack. In our party, Thiel had clearly assumed the alpha position. Had he been a wolf, his tail would have
been flying high as he set a fast pace through the woods, stopping
only occasionally to bark his position back to us.

Half a mile or so in, we broke through the alder into a bright
spruce swamp. Thiel paused suddenly in a clearing where the snow
cover was rumpled. He picked up a piece of bone lying there. Cor-
doning off the area with outstretched arms, Thiel started thinking
out loud:

"It wasn't a deer kill. A fresh kill leaves too much pink snow. This
was a single wolf just passing through when it got a whiff of something familiar. Over here." He indicated where the snow had been
dug from under a bush, a possible scent post. "The wolf had cached
a deer leg from an earlier kill beneath the snow here and remembered it when he sniffed the bush."

Thiel stooped and retrieved a leftover, a pair of fawn hooves, ex-
quisite as tortoiseshell. He slipped them into his pocket and
headed back to the truck. Not a few hunters take a dim view of the
wolf's return to Wisconsin, because it's a rival predator. But a wolf
will normally take one deer every sixteen days, or about twenty-five
a year, if he eats only deer—a minuscule cut of the venison.

Near Moose Junction we stopped to eat lunch on the warm hood
of the truck. Thiel leaned back against the windshield. He said he
was getting spring fever. He was anxious to trap again, particularly
after losing number 1187.

When Thiel first set his traps near here, in May 1980, he worked
with a young federal trapper from Minnesota. In twenty days they
caught a lot of small animals and five timber wolves. One of these

was a lanky yearling male, cinnamon colored, with a gray-and-white underside. They immobilized the wolf using a dart loaded with ketamine hydrochloride, a muscle relaxant, examined him, tagged his ear with his number, and attached a radio collar around his neck.

"He was a real adolescent," Thiel said, "a gawky wolf with a skinny frame and big feet. Always off by himself."

"Within a pack, wolves have a definite personality range, but the wolves with collars are the only ones you really get to know. Everyone I work with knew 1187. All the pilots knew him. He had such a big range, over a hundred square miles, and he wandered over all of it. Sometimes he'd trespass into another pack's territory and get kicked out. I worried about him because of the unwolfish things he'd do, like walking up to a pulp cutter, or trotting along a state highway a week before deer season. The big dope."

Thiel spoke with a mixture of irritation and affection, like a coach appraising a clumsy recruit with great potential. He had high expectations in regard to 1187. The wolf had been acting like an alpha male, not squatting to urinate, as subordinates do, but raising his leg to do it into the wind and assert his independence. This fact and the wolf's far-ranging habits led Thiel to believe 1187 had been ready to mate and form the nucleus of a new pack. But he was gone now, and with him the best-laid plans.

"I knew he was going to get it," Thiel said, "and darned if he didn't."

The next morning the pilot called to say the ceiling was too low for him. Thiel was disappointed that he couldn't fly. On the ground he wouldn't sight any wolves; he'd have to be content with what they'd left behind.

They hadn't left much. The snow cover on Empire Swamp Road was crusting over. The clearest sign we came upon were our own footprints, which we'd made a few days before when we'd stopped for lunch.

Before checking out the Bear Lake pack, Thiel decided to stop to visit a farmer who had reported wolf tracks beside his cattle pasture. Alonzo Melton has a nice spread, 120 acres, mostly wooded, and it sits squarely on the boundary between two of Thiel's wolf packs. Melton wasn't home. His son led us through the snow to the north forty, where ten Herefords were pastured, some apparently ready to calve. A few feet from the fenced cattle we startled crows feeding on a frozen gut pile, dumped after a butchering last fall. Animal tracks radiated from it like spokes on a wheel. One set was large and led into the surrounding forest. Thiel followed it a ways. When he returned he said simply, "They're wolf all right."

A documented case of wolf predation hasn't occurred in Wisconsin since 1976, when several sheep were killed about ten miles from the Melton farm on the Tamarack River. But if the wolves take hold, Thiel knows that relations with livestock farmers could become strained, as they have in northern Minnesota, where wolves are numerous and are classified as threatened rather than endangered.

When we returned to the farmhouse, Melton was waiting by the back porch. Thiel told the farmer he could avoid some "potential wolf trouble" if he'd move the gut pile and bring in his cows when they were ready to calve.

Melton stood there doing a slow burn. He, in turn, had some advice for Thiel. He wanted the wolves trapped off his property, and he wanted them moved "real soon."

"Look," he said, "the deer are gone. The hunting's no good around here since the wolves moved in. And now that they've wiped out the deer, they'll come after my cows."

Thiel was looking skeptically at the head of a six-point buck propped on a woodpile. He told Melton that the state couldn't remove a wolf until there was an actual case of livestock predation. And he added that Wisconsin, unlike Minnesota, pays no compensation for wolf-killed livestock.

We seemed to be frozen in a familiar scenario: homesteader

against bureaucrat. But the roles seemed miscast, the lines of opposition sharper than they needed to be.

"Look, I love wild animals," Melton said, "maybe more than you do. That's why I moved up here. But I need them cows to make a living."

Thiel tried to meet him halfway. He admitted that the law put the farmer in a tough position, and said that he would keep an eye on Melton's farm to see if any more wolf tracks appeared.

Slowly the scenario dissolved. As we left, Melton suggested that someday Thiel stop to talk to his neighbor, who also raised livestock.

"Only he isn't likely to be as receptive as me," Melton said.

Thiel didn't stop at the other farmhouse but drove on to Bear Lake Road to look for tracks. He was especially interested in locating a female that had been with 1187 the night he was shot. A week before, a couple living in a lakeside cottage had awakened to their dog's barking. As isolated people will do, the man went to the door with a rifle in his hands. He saw a doglike figure at the end of his dock and raised his rifle. Later he would say he thought he was shooting at a dog that had been running deer.

As the cottage door opened, 1187 left the dock and walked north a short distance along the lakeshore. When the door slammed, the wolf turned back to face the noise. The bullet entered its sternum and tore through its heart. A second wolf, which Thiel believes may have been 1187's potential mate, ran off across the lake. The man fired again but missed. When he saw the black radio collar and ear tag on 1187, he drove to the nearest phone, called the warden and said he'd mistakenly killed a wolf.

Despite setbacks like this and those years of doing unpaid, unofficial research, Thiel considers himself lucky, because Wisconsin is now studying wolves and he is in charge of the project. He goes about his work furiously, for fear that his luck will soon disappear, because federal wildlife research funds have been cut and state money is running out.

Before turning in on the last night of my visit, Thiel suggested that we do a little howling. Why not? We drove down a dark back road, close to a sighting Thiel had made from the air that morning.

In summer Thiel howls to locate a pack, knowing he's found it when the responding howls are accompanied by the higher-pitched yips of pups. One needn't sound like a wolf to elicit a response; some biologists make contact using a siren. But Thiel wants to sound like the real thing. He has practiced howling in his bedroom to a recording of wolf howls, as if it were one of those Berlitz discs that teach how to speak a foreign language.

Out on the road Thiel let out a low growl that quickly climbed several octaves into a long, long, hurtful wail that filled the woods and left me disquieted. There was no response. He supposed that the pack had moved on. But he tried three more times. The last howl struck me as particularly plaintive, laden with greetings and apologies across species lines, and all the more moving for the silence that followed.

Wolf Redux

When I'm cross-country skiing, I like to keep my eyes on the ground to see what's passed this way before me. Animals lay out trails along the contours of hills exactly as a person would to minimize slope and effort. Like us, they seek the path of least resistance. Sometimes I'd descend into a hollow where so many animal tracks converged in snow that it suggested, during hours of darkness, heavy traffic. I was skiing a trail through the Flambeau River State Forest, 90,000 acres of mixed pine and hardwoods along the North and South Forks of the Flambeau River in north-central Wisconsin. After herringboning up a hogback ridge, I could look out at the spar tops of white pines above a bare canopy of hardwoods. Beyond them lay a line of blue hills that defined the course of the North Fork. Then it was a quick, curving descent through stands of birch and aspen to the river. The temperature was climbing into the upper twenties; already a lead of black water had opened in the ice.

In a few miles I'd crossed the fleur-de-lis tracks of ruffed grouse and heart-shaped hoofprints of whitetail deer on the ridges and tracks of snowshoe hare and coyote in the cedar swamps. I'd also seen fisher tracks and the manlike footprints of a young black bear evidently roused by the mild February weather. Tracks in the snow form a two-dimensional map of animal ranges, chance encounters, and extraterritorial movements. The sheer diversity of tracks also suggests a forest that is not the fixed residence we might imagine but a neighborhood in constant flux. The five-toed tracks of the fisher, a member of the weasel family trapped out of the state in 1932 and reintroduced thirty years later, foretell a decline in porcupine, the fisher's main prey. Pine marten have also made a comeback after a long absence, and an occasional moose will drift down from Michigan's Upper Peninsula to spend the summer wading in a tamarack swamp. But I hadn't come across tracks of what I was most looking for.

In my knapsack I carried a map on which Adrien Wydeven, a DNR biologist and wolf specialist, had drawn four large circles to indicate the location of wolf packs within the Flambeau River State Forest. The ski trail squarely divides the territory of the Price Creek Pack and that of the Thornapple River Pack, which makes sense given that wolves will use topographical features such as rivers for boundaries. Canoeing on the Thornapple River one autumn, I'd found an abandoned den site in the cellar hole of an old homestead. The wolves had moved on but left behind signs of occupation: a thick mat of deer hair, cracked marrow bones, and sun-bleached scat.

Twenty years ago, when I first wrote about the return of the timber wolf to Wisconsin, the fledgling population of thirty or so wolves was concentrated mainly in the northwestern corner of the state near the border with Minnesota, a neighbor with a large and stable wolf population from which the newcomers likely dispersed. It was assumed that Wisconsin would follow suit. But instead of growing, the state's wolf population plummeted by half in the mid-1980s, largely due to *Canine parvovirus*, a particularly lethal disease to pups. Wildlife biologists began to track radio-collared wolves to their dens in order to inoculate pups against the disease. Apparently the intervention succeeded as the number of wolves in the state climbed steadily to over two hundred by the year 2000, distributed in fifty-four packs across northern and central Wisconsin, so many that the species is slated for de-listing from endangered species status, a move that would allow greater management options, including killing of problem wolves. The Flambeau River cuts through the heart of the state's resurgent wolf population.

All this is in sharp contrast to the rather elegiac chapter Aldo Leopold wrote in *Sand County Almanac* on the Flambeau, which his father had praised as the premiere river of the north woods. "When I finally launched my canoe on this legendary stream, I found it up to expectations as a river, but as a wilderness it was on its last legs." By the time the state forest was created in 1930, nearly all the white pine and hemlock had been cut and floated downstream to be milled, so it was a ragged, second-growth forest Leopold drifted past in his canoe a decade later. All that tied the river to its wilderness past was the rumor that a "wolf or two still roams the upper Flambeau." Then in 1954 the last vestige, a 93-pound wolf, was trapped along Price Creek, not far from here. A few years later the state finally removed the bounty on wolves, but the reprieve came too late. Wisconsin's wolves were gone, extirpated.

Skiing down the trail, I kept looking for wolf tracks, so intently that I missed a curve and smacked into a snowbank. Finally, on the Pinery Grade, a sunken railroad grade from logging days, I spotted the telltale tracks, twice the size of a coyote's, crossing and recrossing the trail. What was the story here? Was this wolf patrolling its pack's territory or interloping into another? Was it a youthful alpha looking for followers or just a lone hunter?

Although some wildlife biologists occasionally still track on foot, most fieldwork is now accomplished from an airplane, "tracking" electronic signals from radio-collared animals. One long-distance runner that Adrien Wydeven kept tags on for several months was a female wolf, nicknamed "Atrayu," which wandered nearly one hundred miles west to Minnesota, dropping down within twenty miles of St. Paul, before moving back east to form, with her mate, the current Price Creek pack.

Wolves are such elusive creatures that I'm content enough with the leftovers: tracks in the snow, scat, scattered bones. I've only seen a wolf in the area once, crossing a county road in broad daylight with the nonchalance of someone's roaming husky. But it was deeper-chested than a husky and more self-possessed, paying no attention to me as its long legs pedaled into the woods.

Wolves are likely to remain in the areas they've re-colonized as long as large tracts of forest remain. Using GIS data gathered from radio-collared wolves, Wydeven and colleagues analyzed potential wolf habitat in Wisconsin—including cover, deer density, land ownership, and roads—to determine the areas most likely to be inhabited by wolves. Not surprisingly, the most favorable conditions were within public forest lands with a mixture of hardwoods and conifers, and that's exactly the areas wolves have settled. Because it lies within a matrix of a million acres of publicly owned forest land, Flambeau River State Forest will likely be designated one of the core areas in which wolves will be protected even if de-listed.

Trees alone, however, don't make a forest wild. When Leopold canoed the Flambeau, he complained of rounding a bend only to spy another summer cottage with its "rustic pergola." I know exactly what he was describing because I bought a cabin of that vintage on the neighboring Elk River. So it's with some guilt when I say that the greatest threat to the wolves is development. The rustic cottage and hunting camp have given way to the towering second home and retirement villa with attendant roads and services. The suburbanization of the north woods is already having effects in the northeastern part of the state where there is similar forest cover but more residential development and, consequently, fewer wolves.

I skied over a footbridge across Mason Creek then stopped at a three-sided shelter to replay the pivotal scene in Jack London's "To Build a Fire." After roasting a bratwurst for lunch, I started up the next slope. Then I was on the downhill side, passing in and out of shadow as the trail descended through a stand of sweet-smelling pine.

A month earlier, I'd skied this loop during the annual Candlelight Ski. It's an easy run though more complicated on a moonless night. A flickering line of candles set in plastic cups had marked the trail as it curved into the dark like an extension of the Big Dipper. Skiing at night is like flying by instruments. You lose the horizon and the landscape reveals itself in terms of gravity: the steady pull of climbing or the stomach-turning whoosh as you hurtle downward. On the cusp of a hill, I'd plant my skis in the ruts then go into a tuck, straining to hear as I careened through the darkness—all ears like a bat—in case anyone tumbled ahead of me.

Now on the final stretch, the one I'd completed without mishap a month ago, I missed the thrill of skiing blind. All that was necessary to recapture the sensation, as I set my skis in tandem tracks and plunged downhill, was to very briefly close my eyes.

Looking for Home

Not long ago, I was driving a rented car down the California coast on Highway One. Route One is the westernmost highway in the contiguous United States, two lanes of blacktop and a swift drop to the Pacific. This trip was something of a return after twenty years, so I was measuring the scenery against my recollections of it. All of it seemed pretty much the same—white stands of eucalyptus, the light flattened out on the ocean, the crush of traffic at Monterey—until I drove past Carmel River Beach where I realized what was missing. There were no hitchhikers.

I was surprised—and a little disappointed, the way people are when they find things aren't as they left them. The movement of hitchhikers along the coast highway had seemed to me a migration as fixed as that of monarch butterflies or gray whales. Hitchhikers had simply been part of the landscape, staggered along the road-side, holding up their hand-lettered placards like Burma Shave signs. Inevitably, they would bottleneck at certain places. One of these was across from Carmel River Beach, a final stoplight before the highway soared on to Big Sur. It was, I recall, a terrible place to end up because of the sheer competition—girls in halter tops, backpackers, German shepherds wearing bandannas. A regular gypsy horde.

Everyone had an individualized technique. Mine was to pretend to be walking. I did a vigorous kind of moonwalk by which my legs shuffled backwards while never actually carrying me from my spot. Movement was seen as its own virtue.

Later, having flagged a ride, I sat in the windy bed of a pickup with several other lonesome travelers. Despite the work clothes, a lot of them were summer sojourners from college for whom hitchhiking was the Grand Tour without destinations. What mattered only was to be embarked upon the journey and open to possibilities, not caring where you ended up. That night, I ended up sitting around a driftwood fire at the mouth of the Little Sur River, watching sparks fly into the darkness and thinking: this is it—The Open Road!

The Open Road has always been what this country had in place of sacred sites and miraculous springs. Americans did not set off on pilgrimages; they hit the road. This was understood to be instructive as well as curative—an antidote to boredom, a fix on what's ailing oneself and the republic. Overall, the advice seemed sound. Feeling boxed in? Run out of dreams? Take a hike.

But as I say, on this recent sunny afternoon, the shoulder of U.S. 1 was empty. The horde had vanished. I might have asked where all the hitchhikers had gone if the answer wasn't so perfectly obvious. They were in cars, like myself, traveling faster, in greater comfort, and doubtlessly between points more clearly drawn. Somewhere along the line, we stopped being migratory. We dug our heels in one place or another and called it home.

Even in popular literature, the lure of blacktop has been devalued in favor of a stay-at-home regionalism. Instead of Kerouac, we have Garrison Keillor. The small-town life that threatened to drive a past generation of writers bonkers has been idealized by this one.

Recently, I was invited to a writers' conference in Sitka, Alaska. Sitka is a very beautiful place—mountains tumbling into the sea—and the people are easy to like. Almost everyone I met wore jeans and seemed to be about thirty-nine years old. I recognized myself in a lot of them—former hitchhikers who'd come to roost in this corner of paradise.

The theme of the conference was "Locating Ourselves in Place and Culture: Ideas of Home and Travel." I was there because I had written a book about traveling down the Yukon River. But nobody wanted to talk about travel. For five days, eight hours a day, we talked about home—what it is and how you know you are there. The topic seemed inexhaustible.

About midweek, Elsie Mather, a Yupik Eskimo who was also on the faculty, said, "You know, where I live people don't talk about home all the time. It's just the place where you do things."

This struck us all like a lightning bolt. Nobody had considered so simple a factor as *work* in determining where one lived. Somehow we'd gotten the idea that home is something you choose to go along with a particular lifestyle.

Alaska is what I call an intentional place. As with other beautiful regions in the West, people don't just end up there by accident. They move with great deliberation, hauling a heavy freight of expectations and inventing their own stories along the way. Traveling down the Yukon River, I always asked people two questions: How did you get here? and Is this home? Nonnatives invariably had a vivid account of how they'd come to be at this particular bend in the river. But many times I got the feeling their present lives were a continuation of that journey. They might have lived a decade or more in the North, but there was still a tentativeness about calling it home.

How do we make a place home? It is a comparatively new question. Home used to be one's birthright, the place you were from, where you worked. Now we choose places like suits of clothes, to express an idea of ourselves. Am I an Alaskan type of guy? Have I got the stuff to be a Montanan? Must I remain a simple Hoosier the rest of my life?

I don't think, though, that we can make a home purely out of an affinity for a certain landscape. Scenery is not enough. We make a place home by our connections to other people—family and friends. Being rooted to a place may be just a euphemism for being stuck there—held down by mortgage payments, kids, aging parents. Having freed ourselves from those obligations in order to travel light, we may find no roots to sink once we reach the promised land.

The birth of children and the death of loved ones always struck me as signs that one was really home. I remember listening to a young dogmusher on the Yukon describe the burial of a friend who'd drowned in the river. The mourners had chipped away at the permafrost until the grave was dug. Afterward, they lowered their friend's corpse into the hole, said a few words over it, and settled down to a potlatch supper. I thought of Margaret Atwood's poem "Death of a Young Son by Drowning" in *The Journal of Susannah Moodie,* especially the line: "I planted him in this country like a flag."

The fascination with identifying ourselves with a given place seems as much a measure of our transitory times as the popularity of *On the Road* was of the sedentary Fifties. We want hometown cafés and old people on the front porch, not interchangeable malls and fast food. We want a sense of home without the ties that bind. We want, in other words, what we've left behind.

On Being Lost

"Midway on our life's journey, I found myself
in a dark woods, the right road lost."
DANTE

Being lost is an experience to be appreciated after the fact. Only then, when the trail has been located and one stumbles breathlessly out of the woods, does euphoria set in, a personal share of redemption that *I once was lost but now am found."* It's exhilarating! You've never felt so alive as the moment when the landscape reverts to trees and mountains and sky—rather than the amorphous thing contriving to kill you. Of course these insights hinge upon being found, for to remain lost is bereft of meaning for anyone, save members of the search party who must carry the sad news back to the living.

Recently I traveled a great distance just to get lost. A friend researching a novel set in northern British Columbia invited me along for the ride. After three day's journey—via airplane, marine ferry, and rental car—we reached our destination. Telegraph

Creek is literally the end of the road, in this case a precipitous sev-
enty-mile cutoff through the mountains from Dease Lake. It is
also a town with an unfortunate history of false starts. The first occurred in the 1860s when the Collins Overland Telegraph Company attempted to string a telegraph line around the world, from
New York to London, the long way across the Bering Strait until
the success of the Transatlantic Cable doomed the project. Twenty
years later, Telegraph Creek, at the head of navigation on the
Stikine River, was resurrected as a jumping-off point for the
Klondike gold fields. The route may have looked feasible on a
map, but not to anyone foolish enough to try crossing the jumble
of mountain ranges, ice fields, and glacial rivers. Cut off except by
river, Telegraph Creek slumbered through most of the last century
as a big game–hunting outpost where wealthy clients embarked
on forty-day hunts along the Stikine or adjacent watersheds for
mountain goat and stone sheep or grizzly bear. Then in the 1970s
a gravel road linked the town to the Cassiar Highway. Now Telegraph Creek awaited the arrival of tourists who never seemed to
make the turn at Dease Lake because the road, with its hairpin
turns and sheer drops to the Grand Canyon of the Stikine, is too
much a goat path for the Alaska-bound RV traffic. So the town
continues to slumber.

And it's such a lovely place. Gold Rush–era buildings with false
fronts lean against the banks of the Stikine while the more recent
modular housing of a Tahltan Indian village has spread out on the
terrace above the town. The Hudson's Bay Store had been built the
year of the Klondike strike and moved from downriver to its present site. The current owners, Dan Pakula and his wife, are ex-
Americans who arrived as squatters with the general rush of back-
to-the-landers about the time the cutoff road opened, but when the
others went home, they stayed to raise a family. They commercial-
fished and bought the Hudson's Bay Store to run as a general mer-
cantile until the Tahltan Band opened its own store. Now the
Pakulas operate it as a café along with guided river trips and a

fledgling Telegraph Trail Internet Society, finally realizing the old dream of connecting the town with the world.

The novelist and I rented a housekeeping unit on the top floor of the old Hudson's Bay storehouse, a tin-roofed building painted white with red trim. Swallows nested under the eaves. Through the dormer windows we could watch the gray Stikine sliding past the cottonwoods. The salmon run had just begun, and the whine of Tahltan boats could be heard at all hours traveling to and from fish camps along the river.

My friend had his research while I had only a vague restlessness. I'd turned fifty that summer and began to wonder how I could still be on the right path when it had lately seemed like such a rut. You begin backtracking over the course of your life, wondering if you made the right moves, staying so long at one job or in one place instead of moving on to the next big thing. Years ago, at a similar juncture, I spent a summer drifting down another northern river, the Yukon. On that trip, I was always conscious of the salmon migration going on beneath the surface even though we were heading in opposite directions. The salmon at least had a clear notion of where they were going. Past fishermen's nets and fishwheels, past bear claws and a thousand other deaths, they navigated hundreds of miles to reach their natal streams to spawn and die. What's most astonishing about this journey is that the salmon's mental map appears not to be genetically programmed but learned. Composed essentially of olfactory cues such as the chemical characteristics of a given stream, the map allows the fish to retrace, in reverse, their earlier passage to the sea. Combining as it does elements of homecoming, sex, and death, the salmon's single-minded run from the sea makes our own wanderings seem, by comparison, almost directionless. And if by chance the salmon lose their way, it's rarely their fault.

Such was the case on the nearby Tuya River, a clear-running tributary of the Stikine, where a landslide above the river's mouth created a "velocity block," a firehose jet of water that kept sockeye salmon from ascending to spawning beds further upstream. A Tahltan fisheries crew was catching sockeye below the velocity block and inserting radio transmitters in a lucky few that would be lifted by helicopter over the landslide and released back into the river so their movements could be tracked. As a result, the Tuya would remain a salmon river, but the vast majority of fish were stymied. Since the Tuya is not a glacial river like the Stikine, it would be possible to stand on the banks and peer down at this mortal drama as through a plate of clear glass. And that's just what I intended to do.

The gravel road from Telegraph Creek, the original "Trail to the Interior," had once been an Indian trade route between the Tahltans and the more powerful coastal tribes. John Muir traveled this route on his second trip up the Stikine in 1879. A trader assured him that "the scenery up the river was full of the wildest freaks of nature, surpassing all other sceneries natural or artificial." He also mentioned a man who got lost four days in this lush landscape and had "feasted on vegetables and berries and got back to camp in good condition." Muir, of course, was the sort who wouldn't consider himself lost even if he was. In his journal, he noted "Toltan" encampments along the river, the Indians catching salmon in willow traps set in the rapids.

The Tahltans still fish the same eddies in the river although they now use thirty-foot gill nets suspended from log booms set perpendicular to the current and drive their catch home in pickup trucks. As the road climbed above the river, the country seemed less like the Far North and more like the West. Dark spruce forests gave way to juniper and sage on bald foothills with stands of aspen on the wide benches above the river. Horses stood in the middle of the road, heads turned in opposite directions, then parted in slow motion around my car. In Dease Lake I'd seen a lanky Indian teenager wearing a Stetson and a black T-shirt that read: "I'm the cowboy your mother warned you about." In the distance, slate-colored mountain ranges overlapped before fading into clouds.

The trailhead to the Tahltan fish camp was "well-flagged," as I'd been told, and sloped into a deep-shadowed canyon at the bottom of which lay the Tuya River. Eventually, the footpath disappeared, but I wasn't concerned about getting lost since scraps of blaze orange tape had been tied to branches every twenty yards or so. The river could only be in one direction—downhill. Besides, there's a certain exuberance to being the only human figure in the landscape; you feel larger than life. Below the foothills, the canyon was terraced in a series of timbered benches. Scanning ahead with binoculars, I spotted the Tahltan crew's wall tent covered with a blue tarp on a lower bench. But when I made a tree-grabbing slide to the bottom, the tent wasn't there. So I hiked back up the ridge, fixed the tent's location relative to the largest spruce, then made straight for it. In the process, I nearly stepped off the canyon rim into thin air.

The Tuya was where it was supposed to be, flowing at the bottom of the sheer fifty-foot drop, but the tent was on the *other* side of the river, something my informant had neglected to mention. The crew had strung a rope across the river so they could clip their boat to it and pull themselves to the other bank. But even if I managed to get down to the river, I could see no way to cross it. Like the salmon, I was stymied.

At least I could go back the way I'd come. Climbing up the steep, grassy slope proved harder than going down, and every so often I had to stop to catch my breath. In another hour, the sun would fall behind the foothills. I didn't find the orange flagging again until the slope leveled off and the bits of tape led, unexpectedly, into an aspen woods. But the trail was distinct even if I couldn't remember it; you might say it was a "beaten path." Then the flagging gave out.

I looked around with new interest. At first, I'd assumed that the mounds of scat, which were becoming more frequent as the trail led deeper into the woods, had been made by horses like those I'd seen on the road. But I had been kidding myself. The mounds were bear scat. I was on a fairly active bear trail. Backtracking didn't help because I couldn't find where I'd made the wrong turn, so I began to jog breathlessly back and forth between the last two points on the trail that I recognized. About this time I stumbled on what felt like a tree root but proved to be a bleached moose skull, its eye sockets staring into the void, and in that instant the woods washed over me like a wave. Now, I thought, I'm lost.

Nothing had happened, and yet there were physical symptoms that something had: a parched throat, a quickening pulse, blood pounding in the ears. What had gone missing wasn't my body (never more obvious than at the moment) but that ongoing narrative that constitutes one's *self.* There was a feeling now of being obliterated by the landscape, what Willa Cather once described, recalling her first experience with the prairie, as "a kind of erasure of personality." I'd not only forgotten how I'd come in but also who I was supposed to be. In other words, my story no longer held; the backdrop had become the story, and I was fast disappearing into it.

To be lost is to return to the gloomy forest of one's earliest Hansel-and-Gretel fears, especially the primal fear of being devoured. If the dark woods in fairy tales represent, in Freudian terms, the impenetrable thicket of our subconscious, then its terrors are chiefly mechanisms of our own design. Sometimes I dream about bears in all kinds of improbable suburban settings: roaming my back porch, staring through the living room windows. But I've also spent enough time in real woods to know the difference between bears and the ogres that populate one's nightmares. My only close bear encounter occurred years ago in Alaska when one chuffed at me when I interrupted its digging in a forest clearing. I never actually saw the bear, only heard it loudly announce itself, like a man clearing his throat as he enters the room. We both made our escape.

The sun was almost behind the hills. I hiked eastward along the edge of the aspen, so that if I had to spend the night at least I could see what was coming. As I did, I began to sing, pitifully out of tune, to announce myself to potential bears and calm my own nerves. Unfortunately, my repertoire is limited to a few show tunes. What might a boar grizzly think of someone crashing through its woods, someone inexplicably warbling, "Hello Young Lovers"?

So how did I get back? Backtracking for the umpteenth time, I stumbled, quite by accident, on the right path. Somehow, on my initial ascent I'd gotten turned around, heading west instead of east, and followed a hunter's flagging onto the bear trail. Once I knew where I was, the landscape reverted to scenery and those nightmare bears shuffled back into hibernation.

My problem, as I understand it now, was in pinning my hopes to the plastic flagging, which proved as ephemeral as Hansel's bread crumbs. A false trail. Instead, I should have made a mental map of the country by incorporating its features into that first-person narrative we all make of our lives: "Here is the aspen where I stop to catch my breath." "This is the bend in the ridge where I leave the trail." Call it navigation by narration. The Tahltans must have practiced something similar as many of their place names are shorthand versions of past events. The long mountain lake to the east, for example, is called *Eddontennajon*, which translates into "Lake-Where-the-Little-Girl-Drowned." A sad story but also a signpost.

On the drive back to Telegraph Creek, I kept thinking ahead, reordering my priorities, imagining myself becoming a better person—a gentler father, a more industrious writer. But back in our room above the Hudson's Bay storehouse, I quickly reverted to the old ways and drained half a bottle of the writer's Irish whiskey recounting the day's misadventure. Then I used a pay phone down the hall to call my wife, two thousand miles away, and announce that I'd found myself.

We didn't have the place to ourselves that night. The owner had rented the room across the hall to a Tahltan wedding party so they could freshen up before a traditional ceremony downriver the next day. At first, we heard shrieks of laughter from the bride and her maids of honor. Then it got quieter. I couldn't exactly hear what they were saying, but the tone grew more reflective as, I imagined, the bride contemplated the great divide she was about to cross into unfamiliar territory. Eventually the party broke up. "Don't say 'good-bye,'" a male voice called softly from the hallway. "Say 'I'll be seeing you.' That's the Indian way."

Good advice, I thought.

In a Far Country

Most of us are some garden variety of transcendentalist, locating God everywhere in the universe if any place at all. We expect spiritual experience to come at solitary and random moments, so the idea of gathering once a week in a certain place to have them has lost currency. It's the individual vision quest now, not the collaborative routine of religious services. Most of my friends stopped going to church in college, where they first escaped their parents' grasp, and even now the memory of dressing up in their Sunday best to sit still in a pew for an hour or more remains one of enforced tedium. But hardly anyone wears a suit and tie to church anymore, and an hour of hymn singing and meditation sounds better the older you get. Transcendence on the installment plan. After a decade's absence, I started attending Mass again, initially to fill the hole on Sunday mornings, but later because I realized that I like going and had missed it all along. I like the liturgical year's slow progression through Ordinary Time toward those landmark seasons of Advent and Lent. I like the familiar stories of moral conse-

200

quence. And I like the habit, once a week, of contemplating mortality—mine and others.

To say the Mass is universal misses the importance of place. Over the years I've attended services in shopping centers, in sweaty gymnasiums, in domed cathedrals large enough to fly a kite; the masses were identical in form but not in the feelings they evoked. My favorite church, the one in which I feel most connected to the ceremony at the altar, isn't my home parish but the one we attend when visiting my in-laws' farm outside Rochester, Minnesota. St. Bridget's is set on a small rise surrounded by cornfields and rolling pasture. It has lancet windows, a gothic belfry, and buff-colored limestone walls with a cornerstone dated 1859. Irish farmers, many of whom had fled the Potato Famine, built the church and named it for their patron saint—a fifth-century abbess known as Mary of the Gael—and hoped for better harvests. A statue of St. Bridget stands in a niche above the front door with a stone cow at her feet. Cloaked and wimpled, she holds a shepherd's crook in one hand and stares across the road at a herd of live Herefords grazing in a pasture. Inside, through the vestibule with its dangling bell rope, the three-foot-thick walls keep the church cool as a cellar in summer and tolerably warm in winter. The names on the stained glass windows—GRIFFIN, O'BRIEN, CAMPION, CONVOY, BURNS—are the names of the people sitting beside you in the pews.

The usher and the altar boy share the same small-boned Irish face though automated dairy parlors will probably save the youngster from acquiring his grandfather's stoop-shouldered gait. Because most of the parishioners are farmers, there are usually three generations of any family crowded into a pew and another three buried in the cemetery beside the church. If a windstorm knocked down all the tombstones in the cemetery, it would look like a plat map of the township, white rectangles inscribed with Irish surnames. The tombstones closest to the church are slabs of lichen-covered limestone with the place of birth marked *County Cork* or *County Wexford*; these give way to polished marble, some with miniature flags, that run in uneven rows to the back fence where a cornfield begins.

Five priests have come and gone through St. Bridget's in the dozen years I've sporadically attended. In memory, they seem as remarkable or as annoying as any visiting uncle who comes to dinner once a week and dominates the conversation. One retired in bad health to play the casinos; another left after sparking a divisive scandal; others were cheerful pinch-hitters, filling in until a permanent replacement could be found. The best, I think, was Father Nintemann, O.B., the last priest to actually live in the rectory at St. Bridget's before the church became a satellite to a larger parish. He'd spent his priestly career traveling around to various churches to give missions, so this was his first real parish and his speaking manner was always a little formal, a little scholarly, as if he was addressing us for the first and last time. His health wasn't good even when he started, and he'd often pause during services to catch his breath, a thin, stooped man standing on the altar waiting for his lungs to fill. The winter before he died, he flew to South America between rounds of chemotherapy to a shrine of the Virgin somewhere in the mountains, a place where the lame and halt streamed from all over the world, hoping for a miracle. Some of the pilgrims may have gotten one, but not Father Nintemann. When he returned, he auctioned off his personal belongings and continued to say Mass though he no longer had the strength to deliver the gospel, the "good news," but sat on a chair by the altar and listened to it with the rest of us.

Every Sunday for most of my life I've listened to these Bronze Age stories and puzzled over what possible bearing they might have on my own situation. When I was a child, the wording alone— "Jesus is stripped" or "the five foolish virgins and their wicks"— could set off a bad case of the giggles. But at St. Bridget's that same language with its heavy freight of agricultural imagery—sowing and reaping, harvest and slaughter—can't help sounding less metaphoric, more matter-of-fact when the people sitting next to you face those same chores once they get home and change clothes.

My favorite is the parable of the Prodigal Son. It's such a masterpiece of compression: the younger brother demanding his portion, setting off to a far country where he wastes his inheritance in *riotous living*, then a famine, the youth sinking to the position of hired man on a hog farm. All this in a few opening sentences! The rest of the story consists of three scenes, one for each of the principle characters, who are simply referred to as the father, the older brother, and the younger son—the family unit minus any females. Plotwise, the Prodigal Son makes a far better story than the two parables that frame it in Luke's Gospel, The Lost Sheep or The Piece of Silver, if for no other reason than the lost sheep doesn't have an older brother.

The promise of the story is that you can always go home again. A comforting illusion, especially when you're young. But you can't leave for a new life and expect things to remain the same if you return. Even the younger son must realize this since he doesn't intend to ask for reinstatement, just some scraps of food. Only the father, the old fool, seems to think time and distance won't matter, that his boys can just pick up where they left off, all of them sitting around a table again and planning the day's work. The older brother knows better.

The most poignant scene of the story is when the older brother comes in from the field and hears music and dancing. Nobody bothered to tell him of the wastrel's return; he had to learn the news from a servant. So he just stands there outside the banquet hall listening to the fun when the father comes out to smooth things over. This is what we're supposed to take away from the reading, the father's perfect love that forgives everything. But that's not what I get out of it. All I can picture is the older brother dutifully listening to the old man prattle on and all the while thinking, *Yeah, but what about me?*

When I was younger, it was easy to identify with the younger brother, who at least had the merit of being a man of the world. Not for him the daily grind when there are new horizons to conquer. But he wants it both ways, to light out for a far country while holding on to the safe harbor of home. There's also something calculated in the younger brother's return, the way he rehearses his act of contrition and accepts the unearned celebration. Maybe that's what I recognize in myself.

I have two brothers, along with a gaggle of brother-in-laws, and given the right circumstances—say, if I've spent a drizzly afternoon repairing a section of my father-in-law's fences—I might be inclined to play the put-upon older brother of the parable, wiping my brow and wondering where the justice is in the world. But never here, not at St. Bridget's where the pews are lined with so many older brother types who stayed on the farm and worked hard for little recognition and nothing by way of promotion. The rewards of farming are largely internal, the satisfaction of making a go of things despite fluctuating markets and zero-return on one's own labor. The horizons you conquer are those you've seen from sunrise to sunset all your life.

Of course, nobody at church has the bad manners to point me out as an interloper, the equivalent of the Easter Catholic who shows up once a year to cover eventualities. When the book I'd written about my in-laws' farm came out, a neighbor, Jimmy Sheehan, pointed a finger at me as we left church, and announced in mock warning, "Watch it! He'll write down every word you say!" But I was already at work on another writing project. Sense of place is one of the shallower virtues of literature because writers themselves are always coming or going to the next far country, so that their *sense* of a place is necessarily second-hand, picked up from people like Jimmy Sheehan who won't be leaving when the weather turns cold or the story peters out.

Sooner or later, if we live long enough, we get to be all the characters in the parable. That's the sad news. It also explains the older brother's resentment and the father's quickness to forgive; they may be remembering similar excursions when they were young and feckless, before the weight of responsibility planted them in place. That's what I get out of the story—this notion of circularity, that life's events repeat themselves unerringly even if we're no longer the ones repeating them, an idea perfectly obvious on a farm where everything comes around on a seasonal cycle. Every spring, calves are born, only to be trucked off to market in the fall. Next spring, the pasture is filled with new calves that seem identical to those they replaced, but they aren't. So it is in church. Year after year, the prodigal son returns to throw the house into turmoil. Sunday after Sunday, Christ dies at the offertory and rises again before communion. Father Nintemann dies, and the next week there's another priest to take his place.

I'm not a very good Catholic, though I try to make up in hope what I lack in faith. Still, I can't resist the appeal of the gospel stories, especially in this place, where their lessons seem so transparent: *We live briefly in the present tense and then forever in the past . . . Either nothing matters or everything does.* Like the insufferable old lady in Flannery O'Connor's "A Good Man Is Hard to Find," I'd be a better person if only there was someone around to shoot me every day of my life. I go to Mass to be reminded.

One of the previous pastors at St. Bridget's had shortened the service by dispensing with the choir and substituting in its place a cheap tape recorder, which he switched on and off at whim to release the somber voice of Tennessee Ernie Ford. Now the choir has been restored, bolstered by a piano played by the choir leader's wife, a dark-haired woman with the sad-beautiful face of a *Mater Dolorossa*. Singing in church, like singing in the shower, is one of those acoustical tricks that can inflate even a paltry voice like mine by mingling it in an echo chamber of other voices until the overall sound is greater than the sum of its parts. The closing hymn is usually upbeat, chock-full of rising notes and *alleluia's* to muster us out the door in a hopeful mood. Even if there's no free breakfast in the rectory cafeteria, people don't hop in their cars right away. They dawdle awhile in the parking lot between church and cemetery, catching up on each other's children and crops. All the things that matter.

Acknowledgments

Most of these pieces originally appeared, sometimes in different form, in the following magazines: *Harper's Magazine, Audubon, Sports Illustrated, Mānoa, Outside, Missouri Review,* and *Harrowsmith Country Life.* Needless to say, the editors at those magazines had a hand in shaping the final versions of what I wrote, but I wish to thank two in particular, Charis Conn and Linda Verigan, for their good advice and encouragement. Thanks as well to Gary Fisketjon at Knopf and Harry Foster at Houghton Mifflin for editing my first two books, chapters of which are represented here. And thanks to Pamela McClanahan at Borealis Books for putting this collection together. Finally, many of these articles could not have been written without people who were gracious enough to share their time and expertise: Joe Bee Xiong, Robert Thompson, Kathy King, Richard Bell, Robert Stone, and Robert Elkins among others. Then there is Sharon, who has been everything—editor, companion, wife.

A Northern Front was designed and set in type by Will Powers at the Minnesota Historical Society Press. The type is Miller, designed by Matthew Carter. The paper is Glatfelter Natures, made with 50 percent post-consumer waste paper. This book was printed by Thomson-Shore, Dexter, Michigan.

CPSIA information can be obtained
at www.ICGtesting.com
Printed in the USA
BVOW03s0216041017
496586BV00020B/27/P